kitten taming

kitten taming

Train your cat's inner tiger

David Taylor

THUNDER BAY
P · R · E · S · S

San Diego, California

Dedication
To Sue Driscoll and her five shorthair *muchachos negros* in Majorca

Thunder Bay Press
An imprint of the Advantage Publishers Group
THUNDER BAY 10350 Barnes Canyon Road, San Diego, CA 92121
P · R · E · S · S www.thunderbaybooks.com

All notations of errors or omissions should be
addressed to Thunder Bay Press, Editorial Department,
at the above address. All other correspondence
(author inquiries, permissions) concerning the
content of this book should be addressed to
Octopus Publishing Group
2–4 Heron Quays, London E14 4JP

ISBN-13: 978-1-59223-986-3
ISBN-10: 1-59223-986-2

Library of Congress Cataloging-in-Publication Data
Taylor, David, 1934-
  Kitten Taming : train your cat's inner tiger / David Taylor
    p. cm. Includes index
  ISBN 978-1-59223-986-3
  1. Kittens. 2. Cats -- Training. I. Title
  SF447.T395 2009
  636.8'0887--dc22
                    2008042428

Printed in China.
1 2 3 4 5 12 11 10 09 08

Note Unless the information is specific to males
or females, throughout this book kittens and cats
are referred to as "he" and the information and
advice are applicable to both sexes.

The advice in this book is provided as general
information only. It is not necessarily specific
to any individual case and is not a substitute
for the guidance and advice provided by a
licensed veterinary practitioner consulted in
any particular situation. The publisher accepts
no liability or responsibility for any
consequences resulting from the
use of or reliance upon the
information contained
herein. No kittens
were harmed in the
making of this book.

Contents

Introduction

If you have already brought a new kitten into your home or plan to do so soon, congratulations! Often underestimated and undervalued, cats make the most interesting, entertaining and attractive of all pets.

If your new cat is to show you the many facets of his character and ability, however, he needs to be properly domesticated, educated, and trained. The ancient, wild prowling hunter that still lurks within all cats has to be tamed, and this is where you will play a vital role, as this book will explain.

Most importantly, your well-trained pet will definitely live longer! Bring up your kitten properly and he will be far less likely to go roaming around the neighborhood, thereby getting into trouble by picking up ailments and injuries. All the longest-living cats I have ever met had been thoroughly trained and successfully tamed by their loving owners.

As you come to understand your kitten's thinking and motivation, you will be able to care for him in a much more comprehensive way than by simply putting down a dish of food and opening the backdoor when he wants to go out. The kitten will be happier, more content, and free from stress, while you will gain immeasurable and lasting pleasure in having this new family member in residence.

your
amazing cat

What is a cat?

Heredity

Cats have been domesticated and kept by humans for thousands of years, both as companions and for their value as pest controllers, but all owners and potential owners should be aware that their cat is descended from a highly successful predator.

Early history

The gorgeous little bundle of fur curled up on your lap is actually a member of a proud, predatory species with a history that can be traced back to five female cats that lived in the Near East some 130,000 years ago. One of your cat's wild relatives, and one that is indistinguishable from him genetically, is the African Wild Cat, which can still be found living in all parts of Africa.

Although the earliest firm evidence of cats being domesticated by humans comes from a 9,500-year-old grave in Cyprus, where a cat was found buried beside a human, it probably began gradually about 12,000 years ago, as hunting, nomadic peoples settled down and started to farm. With farming came the cultivation of grain and, naturally, grain stores. In due course small wild cats began to move in from the countryside to prey on the rats and mice that also relished grain. Humans quickly came to recognize the value of having such effective rodent operatives around.

The cats' status in human society changed dramatically some 6,000 years ago when Egypt, at that time the most important country of the Middle East, began venerating these useful creatures as semi-divine aspects of the sun god, Ra, and the goddess of fertility, Bast.

Of course, even today there are millions of people around the world (undoubtedly including you and I) who, in their own way, continue to adore, if not venerate, their cats!

Cat breeds

The development of the many different breeds of domestic cat we see today came about through cat lovers gradually selecting and crossbreeding individuals from the ordinary domestic types that had been around for thousands of years. Although there are records of cat shows being held in England as early as the 16th century, breeding for show purposes did not really take off until the late 19th century. In 1871 a major show for Persian and British Shorthair types was held in London at the Crystal Palace, and at about the same time the first American cat show, for Maine Coons, took place in New England.

Your kitten's fascinating body

Feline physique

Your kitten may not look much like a lord of the jungle, but he is built with the same equipment as a tiger or leopard. As an essentially predatory carnivore now adapting to the easy life that awaits him in your family home, his body is still designed for life in the wild.

Teeth

A cat's teeth are miniature versions of a lion's, and the space between the fangs (canine teeth) is, again like a lion's, just right for them to be inserted precisely between two adjacent cervical vertebrae of his favorite prey, thereby breaking the neck. Where lions' fangs are spaced perfectly for killing gnus and zebras, your kitten's teeth are positioned with mice very much in mind. A cat's side and back teeth are designed for slicing meat, and grinding-type chewing is not possible.

Eyes

Although it's often said that cats can see in the dark, they cannot see in absolute darkness. However, in dim light their eyes do work far better than ours do. This is not only because the cornea, pupil, and lens of their eyes are relatively much larger than ours, but also because there is a special light-conserving sheet of glittering cells lying behind the retina, which acts as a superb mirror. This sheet is what gives your kitten's eyes a gold or green shine when they are caught in a light at night.

Whiskers

It is thought that the whiskers are associated with touch and that they act as sensitive, fast-acting antennae in darkness. Some scientists think that cats can bend their whiskers downwards to help guide them when they are bounding over rough ground at night.

Paws

Look closely at your kitten's feet. You will see that one pad, which lies behind and above the other pads, does not come into contact with the ground. Although it's not certain exactly what it does do if it's not a shock absorber like the other pads when the cat moves around, it's thought that it is an anti-skidding device, which comes into play only when the cat lands from a jump.

Sense and sense-ability

The five senses

Their highly developed senses mean that even young kittens are perfectly equipped to be aware of the world around them.

Sight

A cat's eyes can cope with very low light levels, which is invaluable for a hunting animal (see page 12). Their binocular vision, also important for hunters, which must judge the range of targets accurately, is better than that of dogs. It is now known that cats can see in colors, but they don't pay much attention to them.

Hearing

All cats are able to locate the source of sounds as well as a human can, but their hearing at high frequencies is far more acute than ours.

Smell

Cats' noses give them a much better sense of smell than we have. Their nostrils contain

about 19 million special "sniff" nerve endings, while we make do with only about 5 million. In addition, cats possess a strange little structure, Jacobson's organ, in the roof of their mouth. This organ is involved in analyzing the chemical content of some odors, particularly sexual ones. When your cat occasionally makes a rather odd, nose-wrinkling grimace, which is known as "flehming," he is using his Jacobson's organ. You are most likely to notice this behavior when your cat investigates a patch of catnip in the garden or a trace of another cat's urine on the pavement.

Taste

Cats are notoriously fussy eaters (see pages 54–55), more so than dogs. They do have an acute sense of taste, picked up by taste buds on the tongue and sent via nerve pathways to the brain. It used to be thought that cats had few, if any, sweet-carrying nerves, but we now know that they do have some and that the numbers appear to be on the increase as cats are bred more and more to share our homes, habits, and, inevitably, sweet titbits.

Touch

A sense of touch is also important to cats, and it's a sense that is clearly demonstrated in the way they sensuously rub and bump against people, other animals and inanimate objects. For a newborn kitten, blind, unable to smell, and with closed ears, a sense of touch is vital in responding to the vibrations produced by his purring mother when she summons him at feeding time.

Nine lives?

Landing feet first

It is often said that cats have nine lives. This odd idea probably arose because of the atmosphere of mystery and the occult that has been associated with these animals throughout the ages.

All cats, with their lithe bodies and physical skills, seem to have the knack of escaping from tight corners and overcoming mishaps, and, with perhaps a little luck, your new kitten will be able to look forward to a long life. The average lifespan for pet cats is 15 years, although many exceed this and a few celebrate their 20th birthdays.

Balance

A precise sense of balance helps cats avoid or survive many perilous situations. Among nature's most accomplished tightrope walkers, they can, without actively considering matters, walk along the narrowest branch or the top of a garden fence. They do this by means of unconscious information signals and commands, which link their eyes, inner ears, and brains. You will notice that your cat's tail helps him balance—like the long pole carried by high-wire artistes—as he uses it as a counterbalance, although even tailless breeds, like the Manx, seem to manage equally well.

Falling

The combination of eyes, ears, and brain also come into play if a cat falls from a height. Working together, they compute and then correct the falling animal's body position so that, first the head, and then the trunk and legs, are ultra-quickly aligned to achieve a soft landing.

Cats that fall from very high places are often less severely injured than cats that fall shorter distances. If a cat falls from a window of a building the injuries it suffers increase progressively the higher the storey—

but only up to seven storeys. If it falls from a window higher than that, the severity of the injuries actually begins to decrease.

This is because, after falling for a distance of about five storeys the cat reaches maximum speed, which then remains constant. The inner ear mechanism is then no longer aware of any acceleration and switches off. The cat relaxes and spreads out his legs like a free-fall parachutist. This stabilizes his descent. In addition, a relaxed body is much less likely to suffer from fractures than a tense one.

Finding the way back home

A brilliant sense of direction

Cats possess a remarkable ability to find their way back home if they inadvertently get lost. There have also been many reports of cats navigating their way back to their previous home when their family has moved.

There are many reports of cats that have traveled astonishingly long distances in making their way back to a much-loved family. A cat that traveled more than 1,400 miles from California to Oklahoma probably holds the record.

Cat nav

Cats are thought to make these long journeys by celestial navigation. Your cat sits regularly in your garden, and his brain subconsciously registers the angle of the sun in the sky at any given time of day. He may be able to do the same thing at night by registering the position of the stars. Like humans and many other animals, including even cockroaches, it is likely that cats have internal biological clocks in their brains and that they may also possess magnetic particles in some brain cells that function as compasses.

When a cat is far away from his home he notes that the sun's position is different at some particular hour and, keen to get back to his favorite place and people, he starts to move. If, when he travels in one direction he finds that the angle of the sun differs to its angle when viewed from his home, he then turns and goes another way, whereupon the angle improves. In this way, by trial and error, the clever cat finds the correct direction and heads off, altering course as necessary from time to time. Once he is close to home, with the sun now in its "rightful" place, familiar sights and sounds take over in guiding him home.

Moving home

This guidance system does not work if a cat is left behind for some reason when a family moves house. Then he cannot find the location of his family, and the safety of his new home. So it is difficult to explain the well-known tale of William Shakespeare's patron, the Earl of Southampton, whose faithful cat tracked him down when he was imprisoned in the Tower of London and climbed down the chimney into his master's cell. Perhaps it was a form of feline sixth sense?

What do cats think about?

Feline deliberations

When your kitten is sitting, gazing out of the window, what is he thinking about? Does he wonder about the next can of food you are going to open for lunch or the big ginger tom that lives next door or whether he should move upstairs in search of a comfortable bed?

Cats don't, in fact, sit and think about past events or speculate on the future, and they must never, therefore, be punished by their owners for something they did a short while ago—they simply won't understand. They are, however, highly skilled in acquiring information, retaining it in their memory banks, and then utilizing it to solve problems. Their powers of short-term recall have been shown to last for some 16 hours; in comparison, a dog's short-term memory lasts no more than 5 minutes. Some scientists believe that their skilled handling of the information they receive via their senses makes them the most intelligent of all companion animals, equal in intelligence to a two- or three-year-old child.

The here and now

Like humans, cats learn by seeing, by imitation, and by trial and error, and if they are really to remember something and store it in their long-term memory, they must do rather than see it.

When your cat has to be put in a cattery while you're away on holiday, he does not miss you. He doesn't sit around moping, morosely wondering why you are no longer there and why he has been subjected to this imprisonment. His thoughts are on the here and now: the food, the staff, and the sights, smells and sounds of his new surroundings. He will spend his time reacting to them rather than daydreaming.

Of course, thank goodness, when you do finally return and come to collect him, he immediately remembers you and makes a fuss of you.

Second sight

Historically, cats have frequently been associated with the supernatural, and nowadays they are still credited with strange powers. They are known, for example, to be

able to predict the eruption of volcanoes, the imminence of earthquakes, and, more mundanely, the arrival home of their owners from work. Certainly their acute sensitivity to sounds and vibrations explains how they are able to predict volcanoes and earthquakes and possibly also their owner's return in a car whose engine noise they recognize at a long distance. Nevertheless, the possibility remains that cats really do have some powers of telepathy.

Sharp claws, sharp brain

Feline Einsteins

People, particularly those who prefer dogs, often say that dogs are more intelligent than cats. However, their only reason for believing this appears to be that dogs are more easily trained and are compliant in responding to their owners' instructions.

Cat lovers know better, of course. Cats can be trained (see pages 88–111), but trainability may not be a reliable indicator of intelligence. Many biologists consider that cats are highly intelligent, partly because of their notable adaptability to the ever-changing relationship they have had across the millennia with humans and partly because of their ability to take control of the events and situations they encounter as independent, leading individuals rather than as creatures that are obedient to the commands of others. This characteristic is not surprising in animals that are essentially solitary, self-reliant hunters equipped with an array of state-of-the-art senses as well as an athletic physique.

Measuring intelligence

Deciding if a cat is more intelligent than a dog will depend on how you try to measure intelligence. This has proved to be highly controversial, even among scientists who are studying different groups within a single species, such as Homo sapiens. There is no reliable objective yardstick.

One disputed method that has been used to make intelligence comparisons involves measuring the weight of the brain and the length of the spinal cord. This allows a ratio representing the quantity of brain matter controlling a particular amount of body to be calculated. Some scientists think that this ratio should be bigger the more intelligent the animal.

On this basis a human gives a ratio of 50:1, a marmoset monkey one of 18:1, a dog one of between 9:1 and 7:1, depending on breed, and a cat one of 4:1.

Critics of this way of comparing species argue that there is much more to intelligence than anatomy and that it is, in essence, unweighable. I agree and so, I suspect, will other cat-lovers.

If you look on the internet you will find lists of cat breeds with their average intelligence graded from 1 to 10, with 10 being the most intelligent. According to one list the brightest cat is that little baldy, the Sphynx, while the dimmest ones are the Himalayans and Exotic Shorthairs. (I have met some exceptionally sharp cats of the latter two breeds.) No mention is made of how these conclusions were arrived at, and these unscientific lists should be regarded with a rather large pinch of salt. You know your cat is intelligent; you don't need a list like this to prove it.

your kitten's arrival

The new kitten on the block

Preparing for k-day

Before your new kitten arrives there are plenty of preparations to make so that everything goes smoothly on the day. There are several items that you will need to buy specially for your new kitten, so don't leave everything to the last minute.

Indoor items

First of all, of course, you will need a carrying container to get your new kitten safely home (see page 158).

Another important item is a cat bed, of which there are several types on the market (see page 159). Make sure that it is placed somewhere quiet, away from the

main flow of human traffic in the household. Of course, your kitten may decide that he prefers a different location for his slumbers when he gets to know his surroundings. Cats are like that!

Your new kitten will also need a litter tray (see pages 94–95). It must be positioned in a quiet area of your home, where your cat can go about his private affairs with dignity and free from disturbance.

Other necessary items include food and water bowls of a type that can be easily cleaned separately from the family crockery. You will also need grooming tools (see pages 46–47) and, even if the kitten has been micro-chipped (see page 185), you may decide to fit him with a collar and identification disc.

Although you will not need them immediately, think about getting a scratching post, pad, or pyramid, and a climbing frame or playpen, which will be especially useful in providing a safe environment until your kitten finds his feet in his new home. And don't forget a selection of cat toys.

If your kitten is to be allowed out of doors when he is old enough and has had his vaccinations, you will probably need to have a catflap installed professionally in a door, window, or wall. Your kitten needs to learn how to use a catflap (see page 102).

Safety first

Check your home carefully for potential cat hazards and also bear some of these points in mind for the future:

- If you have an open fire, do you have a protective fireguard?
- Are there any valued or valuable objects, such as ornaments, within reach of an agile, climbing, and inquisitive kitten?
- Are there any plants, indoor or outdoor, that are dangerous or toxic for cats (see pages 128–129)?
- Are all electric cables inaccessible? If not, you will have to disconnect the power when the equipment is not in use.
- Have you a guard for hotplates and burners on the stove?
- Are all rubbish bins inaccessible?

Remember to keep sharp utensils, small objects, and plastic bags where your kitten cannot reach them. Keep the oven, fridge, freezer, washing machine, and dishwasher doors closed at all times, to prevent your kitten climbing in and becoming trapped.

Get that kitten!

The great day has arrived

The day when you are able to collect your new kitten finally arrives. You will be full of excitement and anticipation about the interest and enjoyment that he is sure to bring to the family.

If possible, it is best for two of you to go—one to drive the car, the other to hold the cat box on their knees. You will need some form of carrying container whether it be a plastic cat carrier, one of the more old-fashioned basketwork types, or a hard cardboard temporary container (see page 158). Line the bottom of the carrier with layers of newspaper or an old towel.

First impressions

This may be the first time you have seen your new pet, particularly if it is a rescue cat, so, before you pop him in the carrier and return home with the little bundle of wide-eyed, probably rather nervous fur, there are some things you must do.

- Check him over for any signs of abnormality.
- Is he alert and mobile?
- Are his ears and nose clean and clear?
- Is his coat intact and even, or are there any bald or rough patches?

Lift up the kitten's tail to see if there is any soiling that might indicate the presence of diarrhea. If you have doubts about anything, ask the breeder. It might be advisable to pop into the vet's office on the way back. In most cases, even if an animal seems to be perfectly fit to you, it is wise to let a vet check him over at some time during the first days after his arrival.

If the kitten has been vaccinated then the breeder must give you a vaccination certificate. If he is a pedigree breed bought from a dealer, you should also receive his pedigree papers.

Make sure that you find out what kind of food the kitten has been eating and, if you can, take some of it home with you.

Going home

Now, you're ready. Put the kitten in the carrier by picking him up gently but firmly, his bottom supported by one hand. Close the carrier's door quickly and fasten it securely.

Welcome home

Your kitten enters his new domain

When you are safely home you have to set about introducing your kitten to the household. This is a process that must not be rushed and that is usually easier when the newcomer is a youngster rather than an adult cat.

Humans first

Put your kitten in a quiet room and leave him alone for at least 24 hours with his litter tray, some tasty food, and water. Make sure he can't escape from the room and give him time to explore thoroughly. Don't let any other pets enter the room.

You should visit your kitten frequently to talk to and make a fuss of him, but other family members should not be introduced until he is confidently relating to you. When eventually they can be allowed in, ask them to wait until the kitten approaches them. It's important that he isn't rushed at by some gleefully screaming person and, in these early days, it is unwise, even for you, to pick him up at every opportunity. Watch him, talk to him, and play simple games with him. Let him try some of his new toys, balls, or a length of string, and always reward his increasingly confident contacts with you by small food treats and praise.

Small children and infants must be supervised when they first meet the new kitten to avoid rough handling of the animal or either party getting injured.

Other pets

After being kept alone for the first day or so the new kitten can be introduced to other pets. Ask another family member to bring the resident pets into the room where you sit holding the kitten in your arms. Carefully control the coming together, and have some food treats close to hand for rewarding good behavior by any of the animals. Reward, not punishment, is the essence of successful new pet introductions.

Other cats may well show antipathy towards the newcomer that can last for days or weeks. Make sure your are even-handed in giving affection to both the newcomer and the established residents.

Encounters between the pets should not last too long during the first few days. Over-boisterous dogs should be distracted by food treats and then separated from the cat. A persistently aggressive dog may need to be muzzled and trained in gentle behavior by reward.

Avoiding cat and dog conflict

A checklist

You will have to take special care when you first bring your kitten into a family where a dog is already in residence. Meeting a new animal, especially the arch-enemy of cartoons, can be stressful for all concerned, so use the following checklist as a guide.

- Be patient. Relative harmony between them and the acceptance by each of the other can take many weeks, sometimes three or four months.
- Make sure that there are sanctuaries and escape routes in the house that are permanently available to your cat. You might consider giving the cat and dog separate territories in the house to begin with, by keeping doors closed, and not permitting unsupervised trespassing.
- Feed your cat somewhere that the dog cannot reach. Cats like being elevated, and your cat will probably feel more secure if you feed him on a comfotable shelf or on top of a cupboard.
- Make sure the litter tray is positioned where the dog cannot start interfering when your kitten wants to use the tray.

- Feed your dog separately and alone. This avoids the risk of the kitten attempting to sample the dog's food. Remember that dog food is not suitable for cats.
- Keep the catflap locked until your cat and dog have worked out an amicable way of living together. This will prevent the possibility of the kitten escaping from the house—perhaps for good.
- When all family members are away from the house keep the cat and dog in separate rooms.
- Until the two animals have reached an understanding and get along together keep the dog's lead attached to his collar at all times, including when the dog is in the house. This will allow you to grab and control the dog if he suddenly dashes towards the cat.

Cat about the house

What you can expect

The fun and fascination of having a cat in the family lies partly in the wide variety of things that he will do, most of which, of course, he will do to please himself.

Watching your cat in his new domain is a domestic version of spotting leopards or cheetahs on safari. Your kitten is a miniature of these larger beasts, and even though, unlike them, he does not have to hunt to eat — you take care of that—he still dreams of going hunting. These instincts are reflected in your kitten's playful behavior.

Having fun

In the home your kitten is a joy to watch when he is stalking, ambushing, and pouncing on prey in the form of objects such as table tennis balls, knitting, or even dropped pieces of paper. And it's all so unpredictable. The arched back and crablike walk appear out of the blue, sometimes followed by a mad dash to attack. You will also see high-speed chases with no target involved and for no obvious reason but playful exuberance.

Then there is climbing. Stairs are negotiated with quick agility, while bookshelves are scaled with only the occasional dislodging of a few volumes. And then there are curtains. Mountaineering up the sheer face of Pike's Peak is nothing compared to a kitten hauling himself up the draped window of your sitting room. Your cat would prefer you to buy curtains of some thick, coarse material, which are much more pleasant and easy to ascend.

Getting to know you

Curiosity, they say, killed the cat, but your kitten will be highly inquisitive and remain very much alive. He will be fascinated with the inside of things—boxes, open drawers, paper bags (especially paper bags), and the like—so much so that he may often be found

actually curled up asleep, completely within one of them.

As his relationship with you strengthens, he will talk to you both by voice and body language and will show you how much he likes and respects you by grooming your skin.

Your new kitten will tend to get under your feet while he finds his way around. Forgive him, and when you have been out of the house relish the experience when you come through the front door of the furry ball pelting towards you with a welcome of meows and purrs, and rubbing himself against your legs.

Kitten's first night with you

Let me show you to your room

Understandably, the adorable handful of fur and bright eyes will be uncertain, even somewhat apprehensive, when he first sees his new surroundings.

Even though you have made all the necessary preparations for his arrival (see pages 26–27) and will not begin conducting family introductions for at least the next 24 hours (see pages 30–31), this first night in a strange house is a difficult one for both of you.

Getting settled

Show your kitten the feeding point and offer him some tasty food. Then introduce him to his litter tray and let him examine it. Begin toilet training (see pages 94–95) at once. Finally, show him his bed. Ensure that it is positioned in a quiet place away from the traffic in the home. Don't over-fuss or handle him constantly. If he comes to you, of course, pick him up and stroke him.

Give your kitten the freedom and space to move about as he wishes. Let him explore while you watch, talking to him frequently in a gentle, reassuring tone of voice. He might well appear rather bemused and start mewing plaintively. This is particularly likely to occur when a newly weaned kitten finds himself, for the first time in his short life, without his mother or littermates close by.

Sleeping with strangers

Some cat owners might not agree with me, but I think it is best, where possible, for you to have the kitten with his food, water, litter tray, and bed in your bedroom for the first night. If he elects to snuggle up on your duvet or, as has happened several times in my home in the past, sleep draped across the top of your head, so what? Don't be surprised if the kitten sleeps only fitfully during the first night in his new home. He will settle in gradually, and after the first night you can move his bed to your chosen location.

What your cat would like you to know

This is normal behavior

If your cat could talk to you he would tell you that he, and cats like him, have not changed their natures during the eons of domestication to the extent that dogs have.

Cats are one of nature's most successful designs: beautiful, talented, independent, aristocratic predators. Unlike dogs, which are pack animals, cats are individualists, which walk alone and which, consequently, make ideal one-to-one pets. While cats are independent creatures, they can also learn to love the company of people like you and me.

Still hunters, cats continue to practice and enjoy the techniques and thrill of hunting. Sometimes people call them cruel because of the way they play with their prey, such as a mouse whose luck has run out, before they finally release it, but they are merely practicing their innate hunting skills at such times.

Cats spend many of the daylight hours simply watching the world around them —

a favorite spot is a windowsill—and employing their keen senses to detect the presence of potential prey. Outdoors they like to lie in ambush under shrubs and plants or up in the trees. Then, because cats sleep on average for 16 hours a day, when they're ready for a nap they will retire to some safe place—a roof or a garden shed outdoors, or a favorite armchair indoors—where, safe from attack, they will snooze. Even then, while he is asleep, your cat's senses remain on the alert and, if an alarm is sounded, he will instantly be awake, ready for action.

As a cat lover, you will know that your relationship with your cat will never be one of a pet that is "owned" by you. A cat's individuality is not negotiable. You should regard your cat as a voluntary boarder in your household, one that chooses to be with you and asks little in return, except food and drink. Unlike a dog, a cat will not remain with you out of a misguided sense of loyalty if you do not treat him well. If, however, you endeavor to understand your cat for what he is, appreciate his needs, and encourage his natural instincts, you will be handsomely rewarded by the way he bestows his respect and affection on you. It is most important to talk to your pet frequently and to learn to understand his individual temperament.

Watch me grow!

The landmarks of kittenhood

It is endlessly fascinating watching a kitten grow. The trouble is that the whole process often seems be over in a flash. Here are the stages to watch out for and when they are likely to happen.

Leaving mother

A kitten can leave his mother when he is six weeks old but no earlier, unless it is for medical reasons. Eight weeks, when he should be fully weaned, is the best time.

Assuming that your new kitten is at least six to eight weeks old when he joins your household he should enjoy running around, know how to wash himself and have begun toilet training. If he was shown the ropes by his mother, he will now begin to practice his hunting techniques. At around eight weeks of age, with all his milk teeth, he will be fully weaned. By twelve weeks his eye color will have changed to its permanent shade and his permanent teeth begin to make an appearance. During these early weeks it is important that your kitten learns to interact with other animals and humans. This socialization period helps him to enjoy being handled and to develop an independence of his mother and littermates.

One day old

Ten days old

Three weeks old

Five weeks old

YOUR KITTEN'S DEVELOPMENT

7–20 days Eyes open.

15–21 days Crawls and wobbles around.

21–25 days Walks.

About 3 weeks Queens that go out of doors start to bring prey back to their litters.

3–4 weeks Weaning begins.
You should begin toilet training the kitten.

4–5 weeks Learns to wash himself and play. Runs.

6–8 weeks Begins to practice hunting techniques; he will learn more quickly if he is able to watch his mother hunting.

8 weeks Fully weaned.
All milk teeth are present.

12 weeks Eye color changes to its permanent shade.

12–18 weeks Permanent teeth start to appear.

24 weeks The kitten is completely independent of his mother.

Fourteen weeks old   Five months old   Adult cat

Have cat, will travel

Let's get moving

Most cats start off by hating cars. The noise, the sudden changes of direction that affect their orientation, and the unfamiliar experience of the scenery beyond the windows moving by extraordinarily quickly are unsettling.

Cats will, however, get used to traveling in a car if you set about accustoming them to the experience in the right way.

Keep it short

Begin traveling with your kitten when he is about three months old. Before his first

journey get him used to the carrying box by leaving it for a few weeks with the door open and some soft bedding inside so that he can explore it thoroughly. Put one of your own unwashed garments, such as a sock or a shirt, in the carrier so that he is reassured by the presence of your familiar scent.

On no account make the first journey with your kitten one that involves visiting the vet—for his first vaccinations, for example. You don't want your kitten to associate that initial experience of the car with a strange place, a strange person handling him, a strange smell of antiseptic, and, worst of all, the strange prick of a needle.

When you begin traveling with your cat, take him on short trips three or four times a week to the shops or into the countryside but keep them short. Remember that if the kitten has not yet been vaccinated he must not be let outside until after the second round of vaccine.

Before you go

Don't feed your kitten before the journey in case he becomes upset and vomits, but do take water or, if you have one of the larger traveling crates, fill the drip-feed water bottle in case he becomes thirsty.

Put the carrier on the back seat or in the space behind the grille in a hatchback, never in the trunk. Fasten it securely in place with the seat belt or some form of strapping. Ensure it is out of direct sunlight. Make sure that the car is well ventilated and that the temperature is neither too high nor too low.

When you get home, take the carrier inside, open the door, and let the kitten come out in his own time. It's a good idea to have a dish of food treats and some fresh water immediately available and give him lots of attention.

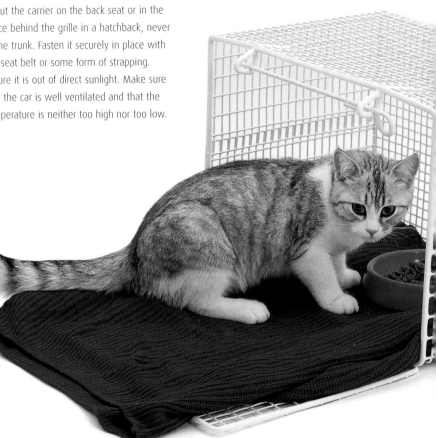

kitten grooming

Well-groomed kittens

Keeping clean

Cats are fastidious about their personal appearance, and grooming themselves—and other cats—comes naturally to them. The process removes loose hairs, unlocks tangles, tones the muscles, and promotes relationships in social groups.

Shorthaired cats

1 Use a soft brush or hand glove to remove any loose outer hairs from the coat of the head and back. With a fine-toothed comb groom from head to tail, moving with the lie of the fur. Then change direction and comb against the lie of the fur.

2 Turn the cat over so that his head is on your stomach or your knee. Turn him gently and slowly by taking his trunk between both your hands. Now groom your pet's underside as before. If you wish, rub the fur with a damp cloth or chamois leather.

Helping your kitten groom himself will prevent the formation of fur balls in his stomach and strengthen the bond between you. You can buy combs, brushes, and grooming gloves in well-stocked pet shops or from your vet.

Begin grooming sessions as soon as the new kitten arrives. Introduce your kitten to the interaction involved in grooming gradually.

Create positive associations with grooming by holding short sessions every day with plenty of tasty food treats. As your kitten grows older you can decrease the frequency of the sessions. For shorthaired cats grooming twice a week is sufficient. Longhaired cats, however, need daily attention. Position your kitten facing away from you if he isn't used to being handled.

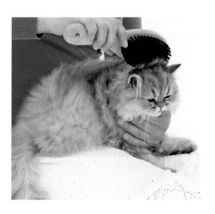

Longhaired cats

1 Brush the cat along his head and back with a soft brush, following the lie of the fur. Repeat several times, and then reverse the direction, moving from the tail towards the head. Untangle any knots, especially behind the ears, the tummy, the groin, and under the tail.

2 Turn over the cat and groom his underside, following the brushing by thoroughly combing both with and against the lie of the fur. Brush some talcum powder into the coat, and brush it out immediately. Polish the fur with a hand glove brush, damp cloth, or chamois leather.

Bath time

Now for some fun

Your kitten may need bathing if he gets some oil or grease on his coat that cannot be groomed out in the normal way. Bathing should be a last resort, because most cats hate getting wet.

Some oils, such as the aromatic ones put in heaters to make the air in a room fragrant, and anything containing pine oil, phenol, or cresol chemicals, such as disinfectants and some wood preservatives, are toxic for cats.

OVER-BATHING

While some cats can become accustomed to regular bathing, you must take care not to do it too frequently. Overdoing your pet's bath times can remove the natural oils in the skin and dry out the coat. Ensure you always use a mild shampoo. Pet shops stock shampoo especially for cats, or a mild baby shampoo can be used.

It's not just that they might ingest them by trying to lick themselves clean; these substances are also absorbed into the body through the skin.

If you find some oil or grease on your kitten's fur and you don't know how long it has been on there, or if you are concerned the cat may have licked it, call your vet for advice. If you know the substance hasn't been on his fur for long, and you are sure the kitten hasn't licked it, then bathe him following the instructions here.

Use the sink or washing-up bowl in a warm kitchen or bathroom with all doors and windows firmly closed. Put a rubber mat in the sink so that he does not slip.

Throughout the whole process be sure to give your cat lots of love and attention and continually talk to him in a calm and affectionate tone of voice. If your kitten objects to be being bathed in this way and you are unable to wash off the substance, then take him to the vet immediately.

1 Fill the sink or washing-up bowl with 2–4 in of water at a temperature of about 102°F. Lift the cat by placing one hand under his bottom while you hold the back of his neck with your other hand. Hold him down with your hand on the back of his neck; if he starts to struggle then hold his scruff.

2 Use a sponge to wet the fur all over, except for the face, and then rub in some cat or baby shampoo to produce a good lather. Rinse the cat thoroughly, using a shower attachment if you have one, or alternatively a cup filled with water.

3 Remove the cat from the sink and wrap him in a large, warm towel. Gently wash his face with cotton wool dipped in warm water. Many cats will tolerate the use of a hairdryer on a low setting at this stage. Once the coat is dry, comb it through.

Kitten à la carte

Feeding your kitten

One of your roles—your primary role, you might think—now that this fantastic kitten is in residence, is to be a provider of good, healthy meals. The problem is that you are also expected to provide meals that an often fussy kitten considers tasty.

Choosing the food

Your kitten may continue to enjoy the type of proprietary food onto which he was weaned before you met him, and all you have to do is keep on buying it. I have known cats that have thrived for years on eating nothing but the same basic food, week after week.

These cats are, however, few and far between. Most cats prefer variety and expect their human staff to provide ever-changing menus (see pages 54–55).

Your kitten's basic diet, and later the one you offer your adult cat, should be one of the nutritionally balanced proprietary foods, of which there are many on the market. There are three basic types:

- Canned
- Dried
- Semi-moist

All three types are formulated to contain correct amounts of proteins, fats, minerals, and vitamins, but each type has disadvantages.

Canned foods have a high moisture content, and some vitamins and minerals can be lost in unconsumed water. Dried foods don't spoil in warm weather, but some cats find them unappetizing. Cats sometimes completely dismiss semi-moist foods.

Little and often

Kittens have tiny stomachs and can digest only modest amounts of food at a time. At six to twelve weeks of age they need no more than two or three teaspoonfuls of food four or five times each day. Gradually increase the amount of food and reduce the number of feeds to two or three a day when they are between three and six months old. Cats that spend a considerable amount of time outdoors will need more food than mainly indoor cats.

It is normal for cats to want to nibble grass. Allow them to do so as it helps them regurgitate any fur in the stomach. You can buy trays of seedling grass for indoor cats in pet shops (see also pages 128–129).

Something to drink

Water must be available at all times. You can offer your kitten milk, but milk alone is no substitute for water. Some cats are intolerant of cow's milk because their digestive systems lack the milk-sugar-digesting enzyme, and you can buy special milk for cats that does not contain cow milk sugar.

Running the restaurant

Waiting on your kitten

When you have decided on the menu that will be on offer at your cat's café, you must now consider how you should organize its service to be best suited to the needs of your kitten.

Establishing a routine

After he reaches about six months of age your kitten should be given three meals a day. If you ring a bell or tap the fork against the bowl or even call his name as you put the dish down in its usual place, he will quickly learn the significance of the signal and come running. Such a system also helps reduce fussiness in feeding. Your cat may, of course, come to recognize other food-time signals, such as the click of the refrigerator door or the rustling of a food packet.

After 15 minutes take the dish away. If it has not been touched, cover it, put it in the refrigerator and offer it again later. Cat food should always be served at room temperature as some cats will quickly regurgitate cold food. When you remove food from the refrigerator you can either wait for it to warm up before serving it or put it (in a non-metallic bowl or dish) into the microwave for 15 seconds. Check that the food is a safe temperature before serving.

Clean, clean water

You might have noticed that your cat sometimes drinks from puddles of dirty water in the garden, or he might even attempt to

drink from the toilet. All this, and you never let the water bowl run dry. This sort of behavior is often caused by the cat's dislike of the chlorine in tapwater. You can overcome this by storing tapwater in a large glass or plastic bottle at room temperature for a day or two before offering it to your cat so that the chlorine has time to dissipate. Of course, if you are really fancy—and I know owners who do this—you could offer bottled still mineral water. Some cats like to drink from a running tap, and if you are feeling generous you could buy him one of the recirculating cat fountains that are now available.

CLEANLINESS

It is vital that all food dishes are thoroughly cleaned at least once a day and that the water bowl is kept full at all times. Do not wash your cat's bowls with your own utensils and cutlery.

Fussy eaters

Foiling finicky felines

Cats can be pernickety, faddy, and fussy over their food. Many owners must sometimes wish that they could take their cats to the supermarket every morning so that they can choose for themselves the flavor of the day from the abundant choice displayed on the shelves.

Cats appear to change their tastes every day. Because their owners wrongly assume that if their pets are not offered some new delicacy they will starve to death, some cats succeed in bullying their poor human slaves into undertaking a never-ending search of the shops and the expenditure of surprisingly large amounts of money.

Variety is best

There are some fussy cats that would rather eat only one kind of food and nothing else—raw mincemeat or cooked fish, for example—but this will not provide your cat with a healthy diet, because single foods like these are not balanced nutritionally. Raw mince, for instance, lacks sufficient calcium and other minerals and also poses the risk of salmonella food poisoning. Too much white fish in the diet can lead to a deficiency in vitamin B1.

All cats must be given a balanced proprietary cat food. Try two or three brands by all means and introduce them gradually into their meals. One thing is certain: your cat will *not* die from starvation.

Signs of ill health

You must, of course, make sure that a cat that suddenly becomes fussy over his food has not got health problems. Sore gums, loose teeth, or the accumulation of masses of calculus on the teeth can interfere with eating. Inspect your cat's mouth regularly and carefully (see page 166–167), and if you are in doubt seek veterinary advice.

Cats that are convalescing after an illness, such as cat flu, can often lack much appetite. Try tempting him with something he does not normally have that has a strong flavor. Some cats love sardines in tomato sauce, others prefer a meaty treat.

Fickle favorites

Of course, one reason your cat appears to be a poor eater is that he is dining out with the neighbors. It's quite possible that someone in your road is accustomed to the arrival at the back door every day of a friendly kitten, which, they imagine, lacks a good home and well-stocked larder. This kind neighbor always has a bowl of chicken pieces or some canned tuna ready for the feline visitor. Peripatetic, vagabond cats of this kind are quite common.

Cat maintenance

Kittens need servicing

Just like a car, a cat needs regular maintenance. It's a good idea, once or twice a week, when your cat is happily snuggled down on your lap, to give him a simple health and condition check-up. Doing this will allow you to identify developing problems early and is also an opportunity to carry out simple "servicing" procedures.

Ears

Look inside the ears to check that they are free from accumulated greasy material or flakes of ear lining. If you find any such stuff, clean the ear by gently screwing a twist of cotton wool dipped in warm olive oil into it. The presence of dark-colored wax may indicate ear mites. Never use cotton buds.

Teeth

Carefully open your kitten's jaws and look inside the mouth. The milk teeth should be clean and white, the gums pale pink and healthy, and the breath should not smell.

If you do find anything that worries you, seek professional advice from your vet or humane society clinic without delay.

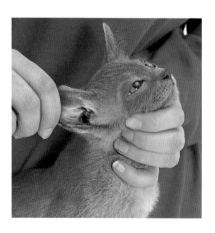

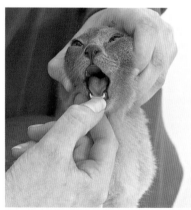

Coat

Begin by checking the coat while you run your hand through it. Are there any bald patches or crusty areas of skin? Are there any tangles? If there are, loosen them with your fingers and use a comb to separate the hairs (see pages 46–47). If your kitten is snoozing he will probably not even wake up while you do this. Look to see if there is any of what looks like fine coal dust on the skin. This "dust" is the droppings of fleas and is easier to find than the fleas themselves, particularly in longhaired cats (see pages 174–175 for information on dealing with fleas).

Eyes and nose

Now check your kitten's eyes. They should be clear, and his eyelids free of mucus or matter. With your fingers and the help, if necessary, of a little cotton wool dipped in warm water, remove any crusty deposits from the corners of the eyelids near his nose.

Are his nostrils clear and free of discharge? Is the nose-pad dry and crusty? If so, pat a little Vaseline or petroleum jelly on it. If your cat suffers from a cracked, chronically sore nose-pad for more than a couple of weeks seek veterinary advice immediately as it can become incurable.

Oh, no! Not the vet!

Vets aren't cats' favorite people

Your newest family member must, sooner or later, be taken to the vet, and your job is to make the visit as free from stress as possible for all concerned.

Absent without leave

Perhaps cats do have telepathic powers because they frequently seem to know when it's time for them to be taken to the vet, and they promptly make themselves scarce. Is it a case of them reading their owner's mind or do they understand when they hear you say, "I've got a ten o'clock appointment for Tabitha at the vet's this morning"?

Veterinary colleagues tell me that people often cancel their cats' appointments or simply fail to turn up without phoning to let them know because they cannot find their pet. A cat that can normally be found snoozing in the greenhouse between nine o'clock and noon each and every day will be inexplicably missing on the day of a visit to the vet. One vet in London has stopped making any appointments for cats because of so many missed appointments.

Getting there

Assuming, however, that your cat is present and correct, there are a few things to remember. Make sure that the cat is familiar and at ease with the carrying box well before his first meeting with the vet (see pages 42–43). If the first trip, apart from the

one when you initially brought him home, is to the clinic, he may come to associate car travel and his carrying box with unpleasant experiences.

First vaccinations

Phone to make an appointment, at a quiet time if possible, and arrive promptly. If you have to wait a while before you are called to go into the examination room, it is far better to keep the cat in his carrier in your car rather than in the waiting room, where there will be the frightening scents and sounds of other animals and humans.

If he was not already vaccinated before coming to you, the first veterinary appointment will be for these all-important shots. At the same time you can ask the vet to check the kitten's overall health and take the opportunity to discuss such procedures as neutering.

If your kitten is going for a second or booster shot of vaccine, don't forget to take the vaccination certificate with you for signing and dating. Keep your cat's vaccination certificate in a safe place, because if you ever have to put your cat in a cattery you will need to present it.

STRESS-FREE VISITS TO THE VET

- Familiarize your kitten with his carrying basket or box well before the first visit.

- Take your kitten for short car journeys once or twice before his first visit to the vet so that he is used to the car.

- Make an appointment at the clinic at a quiet time if at all possible.

- Arrive promptly and keep the kitten in his carrying container in the car until you are called into the examination room.

- If your kitten has already been vaccinated, take the vaccination certificate with you to the appointment.

you and
your cat

Pay attention

Cat chat

Cats talk a lot, not just by vocalization, but also by means of their body language, facial expressions, touch, and behavior. By listening to and observing your kitten you will become an expert in his own special language.

Cats' voices range from angry screeches, hisses, and spitting, through complaining wails and plaintive meows to seductive and contented purrs—experts recognize 16 different vocalizations—and many cats utter a special *zsa-zsa* sound when they spot a bird.

Body language

A cat's body language is highly expressive. The ears of an aggressive cat are pricked and furled back, and the cat carries his tail low and close, bristling and swishing it. A defensive cat, on the other hand, arches his back and turns his body sideways, with the tail arched and bristling. A submissive cat cringes close to the ground, ears and fur flattened and his tail thumping the ground.

Pay attention to your kitten's head. The ears will be held erect and pointed forwards when he is alert and interested, but they will be flattened against his head when some

form of confrontation occurs. In an aggressive animal they are usually presented with a forward rotation but will be folded downwards and sideways if the cat is seeking to avoid trouble.

A cat's tail language is particularly eloquent. A slow, graceful sweeping indicates contentment. An upright tail, particularly when the tip is bent, signals friendship and is often used together with body rubbing, another indicator of friendly intentions. Rapid tail movements commonly accompany agitation and emotional stress.

Cats use touch as an important means of communication with other cats and with humans. As well as sensuously rubbing their bodies or pressing their noses against us, they bump us with their foreheads in order to express their affection or, most frequently, to indicate that they want something—usually food.

The eyes have it

Your cat's eyes convey messages, too. The eyes of defensive and submissive cats show dilated pupils, although large pupils are also displayed by excited but unfrightened cats—as, for example, when they are playing. The pupils of an aggressive cat narrow to vertical slits.

Slow blinking of the eyes is a sign of a happy and relaxed cat. Cats that blink directly at their owners are often seeking reassurance. Avoid staring, unblinking eye contact with your cat because he will find gazes of this kind, whether from humans or other cats, disturbing and potentially confrontational.

Cat confidential

Stop talking to your cat and listen

All cats have several rather sophisticated ways of communicating with one another and with the humans in their lives, although some of these are so subtle that humans cannot register, far less understand, them.

Reading the signs

Some cat signals, like scent deposits, are impossible for humans to understand. Although we immediately recognize the strong, unmistakable smell of tomcat urine, left to tell everyone that this is the top cat in

the neighborhood, our feeble noses cannot even pick up the smell of the more subtle messages that cats leave by rubbing and scratching let alone understand what they mean to other cats.

We can, of course, tell from a cat's behavior when he is cross. If you tread on his tail, for example, he will make his feelings perfectly clear by hissing or screeching. If he has been particularly offended, then a quick bite or scratch of your leg will gain your attention immediately.

There can be few owners who don't learn to recognize that their cat is hungry when he goes to stand in the place where his food bowl is normally put down and stares first at the bowl and then at you. His tail goes up and, if you are in the kitchen and open the cupboard in which you keep the cat food, he will rub or bump against you to encourage you to open a can or take down the packet of his food.

Old green eyes

Cats can be possessive of their owners and can display jealousy at times. In a household with a new baby, for example, it's important to continue to show your cat the same level of attention and affection that he enjoyed before the baby's arrival.

They can also be jealous of other cats in a household, and will show their displeasure if you lavish attention on the other cat by being tetchy and standoffish with you, sometimes growling and going away when you call him. It probably makes him feel better if he whacks the other cat and perhaps bites him, but you need to be aware of the potential for this type of behavior in a multi-cat home. You can avoid displays of jealousy by remembering that your cat is a senior member of the family, who was in the house before the other cat or the baby, and give him extra love and feed him first, treating him, in fact, as you did on the day he first arrived in your home.

Cuddle that cat

Close encounters of the kitten kind

It is important that your kitten becomes accustomed to being handled from an early age. Handling—hands-on contact with your cat—is a crucial part of establishing a great relationship between the two of you.

Some cats enjoy being picked up and cuddled, but they must feel comfortable and secure. Follow the instructions here and remember to always handle your kitten gently and with respect. Avoid grabbing him or over-fussing him.

Picking up a kitten

Resist the temptation to pick up your new kitten at each and every opportunity. You must let him have the time and space to do what he wants—to go and explore or to have a little snooze. Young children in particular can cause problems in this regard.

Never pick up your young cat by the scruff of his neck and don't lift him under his "armpits" and let him dangle. (Getting hold of a cat by the scruff of his neck is, however, acceptable as a way of lifting a cat that has suffered an injury to his body, particularly a fractured limb.) Kittens always need to be handled carefully because their bones, particularly those forming the rib cage, are very soft and are easily damaged by rough handling at an early age.

The correct way is to place one hand around his stomach and the other hand under his bottom. He can then be set down on the palm of one hand while the other supports his head and upper body by gently

Picking up a cat

As he grows older you can pick him up by placing one hand under his front legs and then scooping him up by pushing your other hand under his rump. Then bring him up to chest level, all the time supporting his weight by keeping one hand firmly under his hindquarters. Once up, he can sit in the crook of your arm with his forepaws either resting on your shoulder or held in your other hand and, with luck, you will hear the soft thrum of a purr in your ear.

A LITTLE RESPECT

The new arrival of a soft, furry ball of fun is met with delight by children, but it is very important that they are taught how to handle their new pet, so as not to frighten or injure him. Show older children how to pick him up and demonstrate the gentle way of stroking, not patting, a cat to toddlers who may be over-enthusiastic in their attentions.

holding him around the neck or under the front legs. If you are carrying your kitten anywhere, hold him close to you. Sit down with your cat in your lap, give him a cuddle, and he may well have a snooze. However, if he does not want to be handled and feels like playing, never drop him from a standing height. Set him down gently, give him a stroke, and offer a food or toy treat as a reward for his good behavior. Carefully pick up your kitten in this way several times a day to accustom him to being handled.

Your kitten kneads you

The foibles of lap cats

You know how it is. You have your kitten on your lap, all's well with the world, and then, for no apparent reason, he begins to knead your tummy as if it were a lump of dough. He might even bite you gently or prick you with his needle-sharp claws. Why does he do this?

Showing affection

Your cat's kneading behavior is an expression of affection that harks back to the days when he lay against his mother's warm body and pressed on her mammary glands with his paws in order to stimulate her to "let down" her milk supply. Some cats also dribble in anticipation at the same time, and this action is usually accompanied by a purr. So, if your kitten suddenly gets the urge to give you a pummeling, let him get on with it.

Biting is a different matter and has to be stopped. The cause may be the cat's attempt to attract your attention or it may be the result of so-called petting aggression. Cats do not go in for lengthy grooming sessions among themselves, so a nibble or two on your hand is your kitten's way of signaling, "Enough's enough. Stop it now."

If your cat's claws dig into you when he is engaged in a kneading session on your lap, train him to retract them. Stroke his paws lightly with a finger until the claws retract, while saying "gentle cat" in a soothing tone of voice and adding his name. When his claws are retracted praise him warmly and offer a food treat. Keep repeating this simple training whenever appropriate, and almost certainly he will learn to keep his claws in. It

usually takes a week or two, although some cats will need several months to respond to the training. All that is needed is patient repetition and rewards of words of praise and food treats.

Teething

Sometimes a kitten between the ages of three weeks and six months bites you, and this could be because he is having teething problems. When teething begins give your kitten suitable objects, such as the special cat chews and cat chew toys that are available in pet shops and online. Encourage him with praise to chew on them and dissuade him from trying out his new teeth on your body by blowing hard in his face when he does so, not by slapping him.

What's happening?

Why does my cat do that?

You've introduced your delightful new kitten into your home, but just how much baggage has this mini-tiger brought with him? Did you expect just a cuddly ball of fur, a fawning, ever-eager-to-please plaything like the little puppy that lives next door?

Solitary hunters

It cannot be said too often that cats are not dogs. Dogs are pack animals, and when they were domesticated they treated their human families as a new kind of pack. Cats are, fundamentally, what they always were: solitary hunters.

Your kitten may have the bluest of eyes and possess a passion for canned tuna, but beneath his fluffy coat lurk the instincts of the wild cats. He will naturally ambush songbirds in your garden and bring in frogs as presents for you.

Cats use a number of communication systems among themselves (see pages 62–63), and when he is out and about your cat will revert to the role of lone predator. The messages he sends to other cats are designed to avoid conflict and confrontation, and they are intended to enable him to stay fit and uninjured for the business of hunting and moving from place to place.

Matriarchal societies

Although cats are solitary hunters and individualists, wild cats, feral cats, and cats that live in multi-cat homes tend to adopt a matriarchal society, where the top dogs are females. At certain times—for sexual activity or when they are out and about in territory that may or may not have been claimed by another cat—they obey the hierarchical rules of feline society.

Research has shown that within groups of feral cats social life is based on a network of grandmothers, mothers, aunts, and daughters living as a unit, with outsiders unwelcome. In your home, if you have a number of cats, they will also establish a matriarchy, in which unneutered outsiders are unwelcome. Multi-cat households are best composed of related animals. If you bring non-related cats into your home, introduce them with care and patience.

Rubbing, both of other cats and humans, demonstrates affection and respect and acknowledges relative status. Status is very important in cat society—indeed, cats could be seen as class-conscious. Mutual grooming among cats strengthens the relationships, and is a method of exchanging information between cats through tastes and smells.

Wise owners understand these relative roles and accept that the relationship they have with one cat is different from the relationship they have with other cats. Tensions between our cat and ourselves must not be allowed to develop or your cat will simply withdraw into himself, become aggressive, or leave home.

Your cat and you

Your cat as in-house psychoanalyst

Yet another impressive skill that your kitten will be able to demonstrate is as a detector of the moods of the people with whom he comes in contact.

Your body language

Cats are adept at observing human body language, and they quickly learn to relate to the various tones of voice of their human companions and to their moods.

They are also extremely sensitive to human body odor. The chemical balance in human sweat changes according to the person's mental state—the phrase "the smell of fear" is a common one—and it is true that perspiration smells differently depending on a person's mood, whether they are feeling amorous, fully relaxed, or scared stiff. Your cat's highly sensitive nostrils are better than yours in detecting any odor changes, and he will react to you as appropriate for your mood at the time.

But I don't like cats

You must often have heard someone from outside your family say, when your cat goes amiably over to them: "How peculiar! I'm not a cat fan, but they always come to me."

I have found this to be a common occurrence, and people who, if not actual cat haters, are at least not fond of them, are often greeted by a cat more warmly than people who are cat enthusiasts.

One possible explanation for this lies in the eyes of the human beholder. People who love cats tend to stare, hardly blinking, at a cat to which they are introduced. People who don't care for cats just look at them with indifference, continuing to blink normally. As we have seen (pages 62–63), cats take an unblinking stare, whether human or feline, to be confrontational, a possible sign of impending conflict, and they prefer, at least on first meeting, a disinterested, and therefore unthreatening, gaze.

When you are having a close encounter with your kitten, remember to blink slowly and more frequently than you would normally do when you gaze into his eyes. When you blink, the kitten will generally blink also.

Cats as landowners

Your kitten's territorial rights

"What's mine is mine, and don't you forget it," say cats in their own inimitable way. The boundaries of their territory, both inside and outside your house, are precisely marked out and clearly indicated to other cats living in the vicinity.

Cats mark out their territory by erecting "signposts" of both a visible and a smellable nature to other cats.

Scratching

Many people think that when a cat scratches things with his claws he is simply sharpening them. Certainly scratching keeps the claws in tiptop condition, but this is not because the process brings them to a needlelike point,

but rather because it removes the old, blunted outer claw sheath to expose the glistening new talon beneath. Another function of scratching is to exercise and strengthen the muscles and tendons of the feet, keeping them fully prepared for action, whether that is doing battle or simply climbing the garden fence.

More importantly, however, scratching leaves a visual signal of territorial rights to the other cats of the neighborhood. In addition, when your cat is scratching, scent glands in the paws release a secretion that gives an additional olfactory signal.

Scent signals

Your cat leaves three types of smell signals: urinary, fecal and those from skin glands.

Your cat urinates deliberately when he is marking his territory and can do so no matter how much urine is in his bladder. Surprisingly, the urine spraying routine follows an

unchanging pattern: the area sprayed and the number of squirts never vary. Spray marking is normally, but not exclusively, done from a standing position so that the urine is deposited at nose height, which means that it can be instantly detected by passing cats. Cats of both sexes, neutered and unneutered, spray mark.

When, as part of his natural bowel function, your cat passes motions, he will always try to bury the droppings by scratching with his hind feet. When the droppings are deposited as territory markers, he will make no attempt to cover them up. Typically, these malodorous calling cards are placed on the tops of fence posts or, more embarrassingly, on your next-door neighbor's lawn.

When he rubs against you or other animals, your cat leaves the scent produced by his skin glands. This identifies the object he has marked and indicates his status to another cat. Rubbing you is a way of showing contentment and acknowledging his relationship with you.

Cats as landowners

growing pains

Cat adolescence

Sex on the horizon

We all know that teenagers can be trouble, and your kitten will achieve sexual maturity much sooner than a human being. You must be prepared for this and for the decisions you need to take for your cat's well-being.

Sexual maturity

Female cats, or queens, become sexually mature at somewhere between 7 and 12 months of age. Male cats tend to be mature later, between 10 and 14 months. Some pedigree queens, such as Siamese, are rather precocious in coming into heat at six months of age, while longhaired breeds generally leave it until they are much older.

A queen will come into heat (estrus) in accordance with a seasonal cycle. The heat period will occur at approximately two-week intervals and will last from two to four days. The annual cycle usually consists of two or

three heat periods between early and mid-spring, with repeats mainly in early to midsummer, and sometimes a third in early autumn. Cats being cats, however, some queens elect to go into heat slightly outside these time periods.

Cats in heat

What do you see when your kitten, now a queen, is in heat? Essentially, of course, her purpose is to attract a male cat. She will normally become much more restless, affectionate, and fawning than usual, and she will also be far fussier about grooming herself. There will be greatly increased rubbing and rolling of her body, and she may well indulge in the rather strident howling, known as "calling." She is indeed calling—calling for a mate. Most characteristically, she will regularly adopt a typical body posture with her front end flat on the floor and her rear end raised high in the air. She will flick her tail to one side, while her hindlegs are pedaling away furiously as if she was on a bicycle. If you stroke her she will tend to crouch down very low.

We shall consider contraception, neutering in the form of castration and speying, and chemical methods later (see pages 80–81 and 82–83), but if you do decide to let your queen have kittens, it is best to wait until she has had at least two fully developed heat periods, which will give her body time to become sufficiently developed to cope with pregnancy and lactation, and will reduce the chances of her kittens needing fostering.

Kittens having kittens

To breed or not to breed

Do you really want your new cat to have kittens of her own? No doubt she would be delighted, but before you allow her to have kittens, think carefully about what will happen to them.

Sadly, unless they are of one of the ultra-fashionable breeds, like Bengals, it is not easy to find good homes for kittens. If you or your close friends cannot give them a home for life, what will become of them? Animal charities are hard pressed to find good homes for stray cats, and as a responsible cat lover you should think about the alternatives.

If your kitten is female you must consider contraception of some form. Just letting her cycle for the rest of her life without reproducing is not an option, particularly as virgin queens tend to develop ovarian cysts when they are older.

Speying

Speying (ovaro-hysterectomy) is an operation to remove the ovaries and uterus that is performed under general anaesthetic. It is as safe as the procedure to remove the appendix of a human being, but there are restrictions on when it should be carried out:

- The kitten must be at least three months.
- Unless there are good medical reasons, no queen more than one month pregnant should be speyed.
- A queen should not be speyed when she is actually in heat because the estrogen hormones circulating in the blood at that time tend to increase bleeding.

Birth control

The alternative to surgical neutering is the contraceptive pill or the injection of a contraceptive that has been specially formulated for use on small animals. It is best, in my view, to use these for only short periods because their long-term use can result not only in uterine disease but also in enhanced appetite, which carries with it a consequent unwelcome increase in weight. They are also usually contra-indicated in diabetic cats.

Neutering

The neutering of tomcats has several benefits:

- It limits the numbers of unwanted kittens and prevents the tom from harassing the female cats in the neighborhood.
- It reduces the tom's tendency to stray and fight with other cats.
- It eliminates the unmistakable, acrid odor of sprayed tomcat urine.

Unless they are to be used for breeding purposes, tomcats should be castrated when they reach six months of age.

Is neutering cruel?

Why should my cat be neutered

You will, not infrequently, hear people say: "I think neutering a cat is cruel." What exactly do they mean by that, and is it true? In fact, neutering has advantages for both the owner and the cat.

The surgery

The actual operations for neutering both females and males—speying and castration—are not at all cruel. Nor are they painful thanks to powerful and safe modern anasthetics. Your cat will quickly recover from the surgery, and there are rarely any complications or side effects.

Birth control for our feline friends is completely humane and caring and in the best long-term interests of all cats. If you have any doubts about this, have a talk with your veterinarian or, better still, your local cat protection society.

The advantages

From your point of view the advantages are that your neutered cat will be far less likely to go wandering away and get into trouble in the future. In addition, your cat—and therefore your home and your garden—is far less likely to be pestered by visiting toms (see pages 84–85).

Neutered cats often live healthier lives. Females are not afflicted with ovarian or uterine disease as they get older, and the incidence of bites from other cats, which often lead to the formation of abscesses, is greatly diminished.

There's that tom again

Fending off unwanted attention

If your new cat is a queen, and particularly if she has yet to be neutered, you might find that she becomes the object of the attentions of the local unneutered tom.

Unwelcome visitor

Rather fancying himself as the stud of the neighborhood, this cat is likely to arrive at your home and proceed to announce his presence by generously spraying his rather pungent urine on your doorstep, windowsill, or, best for him if he can gain access, indoors. He is interested in, indeed set upon, sex, and your new female kitten, now in heat, is for him an available female that he has detected as living in his adopted territory.

Such toms are usually very persistent in pressing their attentions, whether your cat is receptive to their charms or not.

Evasive action

What should you do about it? Obviously having your queen speyed will reduce her attractiveness to these male cats, but, knowing there is a newcomer in the form of a young female cat in your house may still encourage the tom to keep on invading your cat's territory.

Try putting some strong-smelling liquid, such as disinfectant, or, best of all, oil of citronella on the places where the tom has been spraying. If he has had the nerve to come in through a catflap, consider changing the flap to one that can be opened only by your cat when she is wearing a collar carrying an identifying metallic fob of the type obtainable from pet shops. Unfortunately, asking the neighbor who owns the tom to try and control his cat's lustful visitations is rarely, if ever, successful.

Visiting felines will get into the habit of stealing your kitten's food if it is made available to them. They may also encourage other neighborhood cats onto your pet's territory. Try to nip the issue in the bud by following the evasive action suggestions given here.

Breed characteristics

The wonderful variety of cats

As your kitten grows into adolescence, you should be able to recognize more and more the particular characteristics he has inherited through his breeding. This is one of the fascinating aspects of having a kitten.

There are Web sites and books devoted to individual breeds, so you can check the characteristics of each breed before you decide what to acquire. There is such a large number of cat breeds that we can look only briefly at a mere handful here.

Longhaired breeds

There are many breeds of longhaired cats, many, but not all, being so-called Persians. They are usually best as indoor cats, and their major disadvantages are the year-round moulting and the need for daily grooming.

Nevertheless, some longhairs, such as the Maine Coon, Birman, and Norwegian Forest Cat, are robust animals with outgoing personalities, and they will relish opportunities to explore outdoors.

Shorthaired breeds

The shorthaired breeds are far simpler to maintain than the longhairs. They tend to look after their coats themselves and need less grooming by you. There are distinct British, American, and European Shorthaired breeds, with numerous color types. British Shorthairs are generally easy-going, placid, and intelligent, and they make affectionate pets. American Shorthairs, while independent by nature, make excellent companion cats. They are usually not very vocal, often mouthing silent meows. Some of the Oriental shorthaired breeds, notably the Siamese, are incredibly demanding, and they are very strident in their vocalizations.

The three shorthaired Rex types—Devon, Cornish, and Selkirk—tend to have loyal characters, and their sparse coats make them ideal for people who are allergic to cats.

The beautiful silver-grey Korat, which originated in Thailand, is both intelligent and sweet-natured. It has a quiet voice and makes a very good companion for children.

The Russian Blue also has a rather shy and quiet character, so quiet in fact, that it can be difficult to tell when a queen is calling.

Probably the most attention-grabbing breed is the hairless Sphynx, a breed developed in North America as recently as the 1960s. These cats are affectionate and cuddlesome, but they do need protection from the cold in winter.

Hybrids

If you have rescued your cat from a shelter or animal charity he is likely to be a hybrid. He might, somewhere among his forebears, have inherited some pedigree genes, but he will be as handsome and intelligent as the most highly bred pedigree. Moreover, having a mixture of forebears, he will benefit from so-called hybrid vigor, and he will almost certainly be blessed with a combination of genes that gives him a longer and healthier life than many more aristocratic cats.

kitten school

How cats learn

Nursery school for kittens

If you are going to tame, teach, and train this cute kitten of yours, you will save yourself a lot of heartache and trouble by considering how cats in general learn.

Experience and instinct

Cats learn both by remembering things that they have experienced (see pages 20–21) and by instinct. Experience teaches them how to jump for a latch to open a door or to gain admittance to the family home by tapping the door knocker or bell that brings his staff (you) running to oblige. Yes, it's true, cats train their owners.

Skills like hunting techniques are mainly learned from the mother and are not instinctive, although some genetic factors inherited from their wild ancestors may be involved. A mother cat that is a good hunter will usually produce good hunting offspring, while kittens born to non-hunting mothers and kittens that have no littermates never learn hunting skills.

Early start

The first two months of a kitten's life are the most critical for the development of his learning and social skills. During this period kittens bond with their fellow creatures, practice copying the actions of others and begin, we hope, their fruitful interaction with human beings. Until you start training him, your kitten will concentrate on learning only those things that are of a practical use in his daily life: obtaining food, the proprietorial marking out of his territory for the benefit of others, locating the snuggest snoozing spot in the house, and so forth.

Play school

Everyone knows that kittens love to play. Certainly playing is fun for them, but it's actually very much more than that. It forms an important part of the learning process. Playing develops the kitten's experience of the world around him and the physical laws that govern it. Through play a kitten learns how to direct and time a pounce, how fast he needs to run after, and at what angle to intercept, moving prey, how much of a thrust of the hindlegs he needs to jump and land on an object some distance away, and so many of the other abilities he will need throughout his life.

When you come to start training your cat, play will form an integral part of the process, and while he learns you will both have lots of fun.

Taming techniques

The basics of taming and training

Many people believe that cats, unlike dogs, cannot be trained. True, you don't come across police cats, greycat races, sledge cats, or sheepcats, but these intelligent animals can and, in some ways, must be trained.

Cats or dogs

Cats in general are far more independent in character than dogs and not at all interested in doing something just to be rewarded with praise from human beings. Cats are materialists, and they want material rewards if they are to learn something. That means *food*. I don't mean that you should withhold a meal until the cat performs correctly. Instead, you should employ food-based treats, although, again, these treats must not merely be portions of your kitten's normal food. Keep a supply of special things that are varied from time to time in order to maintain his interest and motivation. Examples of such delicacies are small cubes of cheese, shrimps or prawns, and pieces of boiled ham. Some kittens may not be as food oriented as others. If this is the case with your kitten, try toys and play as an alternative reward.

Early learning

Your training should begin as soon as the newcomer arrives in the house. Get him used to set routines in his daily life, and try to feed and groom him and provide training sessions at regular times during the day.

When embarking on training your kitten, remember that the approach you take depends very much on his personality. In the early days, your aim is to accustom your kitten to playing with you and interacting with people: it should always be fun. A timid kitten will not respond to training in the same way as a more sociable kitten and you should stop the training session immediately if you sense your cat is stressed or in any discomfort. Remember, training and play should always be an enjoyable experience, for both of you.

Some training will be "positive"—learning to use a litter tray and catflap and answering to his name, for example. Other training will be "negative"—dissuading him from climbing curtains or scratching the doorpost.

When your kitten has reliably mastered the basics, you might think about training him to perform simple tricks, like begging.

As you might imagine, your most important contribution to the entire process of training your kitten is unlimited amounts of patience. But I guarantee you will get results!

Potty training for cats

Outdoors and in

All members of the cat family are by nature clean and neat when going about their ablutions, but in order to be so as pets they must have access at all times to the outdoors by way of a catflap or to a litter tray or trays within the house.

Early start

Begin potty training a young cat as early as possible, ideally when it is three to four weeks of age and beginning to eat solid food. Most kittens are easy to train, as they will normally have watched their mother using a litter tray. It is easy to spot when the kitten wants to urinate: he will crouch, usually with his tail raised, staring ahead with a preoccupied, faraway look in his eyes. When you see this, grab him firmly but gently and pop him onto the litter tray.

If, occasionally, he beats you to it and makes a mess on the carpet, never rub his nose in it. This practice is unfair as your kitten will not necessarily associate the punishment with the crime. Thoroughly clean the soiled area with disinfectant (avoiding ammonia) to remove odors and stains. As with other forms of problem behavior, never smack or hit your cat if he does soil in the wrong place.

For the first few days after the kitten arrives in your household, put him on his litter tray at regular intervals. He will quickly get the idea.

Using the tray

Although most cats are perfectly happy with a simple tray, you can buy litter trays with hoods, and many cats, particularly nervous ones, prefer them. The hoods also reduce the escape of unpleasant smells. These are available online or in pet shops.

Line the tray with newspaper or a proprietary plastic liner and add a layer of litter, about 1½ in deep. Pine wood pellets or peat moss are better than sawdust. Many nervous or insecure cats are happiest using the clumping-type litter.

Position the tray so that it is easily accessible, and, if possible, avoid moving it around, as this will confuse your kitten.

Clean the litter tray every day and disinfect it once a week, using any domestic disinfectant, remembering to avoid those containing phenolic or coal tar chemicals, which are toxic for cats and can be absorbed through their skin.

For advice on tackling breakdowns in toilet training, when cats that have hitherto shown impeccable behavior start inexplicably soiling in the house, see pages 116–117.

LITTER TRAYS

Cats that live permanently indoors or those that are confined for long periods during the day or night must have access to a litter tray or trays.

Outdoor trips

Going outside for the first time

It is best to keep your new kitten indoors at all times for the first two or three days after his arrival. After that, the simple training that involves accustoming him to more of the world around him can begin.

First steps

As long as the weather is reasonable and most certainly not raining, you can let your kitten out into the garden or backyard under your careful supervision. Before his first excursion check for any potential cat

hazards—toxic chemicals such as pesticides and sharp garden implements, for example—and if you can fix mesh, preferably of the stout plastic kind used for climbing plants, along the top of walls and fences to inhibit escape attempts and possible disappearance, which might happen before he has completely adopted his new home. Once your kitten is fully settled in, such defenses can be removed from your garden.

Some of the plants that are toxic for cats are listed on page 129. Your kitten will probably not chew or lick these dangerous species, but it does occasionally happen, and so preventing potential poisoning depends on your vigilance from day one.

Supervise your kitten's first outdoor trips by staying in the garden with him. It is a good idea to schedule these trips for just before mealtimes, so that when you both return indoors he has something to look forward to. In addition, to reinforce his

appreciation of the joys of being indoors again, give him a small food treat or two.

Make sure that all family members are aware that certain chemicals, in particular some ant killers and pesticides, are toxic to cats and must not be used on your premises.

PONDS

As well as adding netting around the top of your fences, you should also cover your garden pond with a net-covered frame or, if you prefer, erect a low fence around it. Ponds are particularly risky for kittens and young cats. If you are considering constructing a pond, avoid one with steep sides. If it has sloping edges your cat will be able to clamber out if he accidentally falls in.

The naming of cats

Who am I?

Choosing a suitable name for your new kitten can be difficult, but it's essential that your cat is trained to know and respond to that name as soon as possible.

Finding a name

Whether you give your new kitten a long or a short name, remember that you need to choose something that you can call out clearly and easily. Single-syllable names are obviously the easiest to use when you are calling your cat, but two or even three syllables seem to work just as well. Sometimes a two-syllable name seems to lend itself to being stressed on the first syllable, or you might prefer to shorten a long name. Pedigree cats often have double-barrelled names and need to be given a punchier, more everyday name. There are dictionaries of names for humans, which might give you some ideas. Don't leave your kitten without a name.

First things first

Getting your kitten to recognize his name is one of the simplest forms of training, and most owners do it automatically, without thinking of it as training.

You should use your cat's name frequently, particularly at feeding and treat-giving times. Use it at every regular playing and grooming session, too. The pitch of your voice is not important; what is important is the repeated use of the name. Quite quickly the kitten will prick his ears and look at you when he hears the word, and it won't be long, even without further "come here" training, before he also moves towards you—unless, of course, he is otherwise occupied in very important

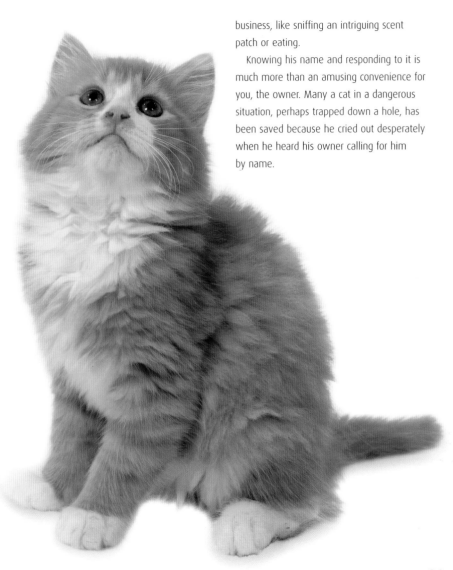

business, like sniffing an intriguing scent patch or eating.

Knowing his name and responding to it is much more than an amusing convenience for you, the owner. Many a cat in a dangerous situation, perhaps trapped down a hole, has been saved because he cried out desperately when he heard his owner calling for him by name.

Positive reinforcement

Training your kitten by reward

Cats, no less than dogs or dolphins, are trained by so-called positive reinforcement. In the case of dolphins this takes the form of fish. Cats respond better to food treats.

Bridging signals

Positive reinforcement means that you give a reward, in the form of a small food treat, when your kitten correctly performs what you ask of him. At the same time, you inform the cat of your satisfaction by giving some sort of signal, referred to as the bridging signal. Usually this signal is a sound or a word that will connect (bridge) the action and reward in the cat's mind.

You will instruct your cat to do something, and when the task is successfully accomplished, you immediately give the bridging signal followed by the reward. A common error in training cats (and other animals) is that the trainer is not quick enough in giving the "Well done! Here comes the reward!" signal.

The sound signal you use may be a word or, as many trainers prefer, a click from a small clicking device held between finger and thumb. These clickers are widely used for training dogs and are available in pet shops and online. Smaller clickers especially for cats are available from most pet stores. As with all training, observe your kitten closely and if he seems at all uncomfortable then stop training immediately. Cats have very sensitive ears so if you find the noise of the clickers frightens your kitten, then try a different tactic.

Training sessions should last no more than five minutes and can be held up to three times a day. Hold them in a quiet place without anybody else or other pets being present. They work best if the cat is hungry, so have enough food treats with you!

Remember that a cat will only ever perform as you would wish if he wants to. No amount of training will achieve results if he does not want to do something.

1 Click and immediately reward without the cat having done anything. Repeat many times. Your cat will come to connect the click signal and a reward.

2 Lure the kitten to you with a food treat and give some kind of verbal command, like "come." Click and reward your cat if he complies. Try this a few times. Now the cat will gradually go on to associate the command with the signal and the reward.

3 Now try it without the food lure and just the verbal command. If the cat only partially complies, still click and reward. You are encouraging him to get things right. Eventually your cat will understand what the command means, and that he'll get a click and occasionally a reward.

The catflap

The ins and outs of life

Catflaps are excellent devices. Not only do they give your cat the freedom to attend to his affairs outside the home, but they also enable you, should you so wish, to control his comings and goings. Most importantly, you can control the unwelcome visitations of impertinent outsider cats.

Using a catflap

Your kitten needs to be trained to use the catflap. He will not instinctively know what it represents and how to use it when he is first introduced to it. As ever, a little time and patience on your part are needed.

The aim, usually not difficult to achieve, is for your cat to see that the flap gives him the opportunity both to explore the great outdoors when he wishes and to return to his comfortable home, with all the food, security and human attention that he knows can be found there. To this end it is important for you to make plenty of favorite food, treats, and fussing readily available when he comes in during the training period.

Do not just grab hold of your kitten and push him through the flap. Cats don't like that sort of handling. Instead, use a peg or piece of tape to wedge or prop the flap open so that he can see the hole and what is beyond and then leave him to go through at his own pace.

The first stage is for you to encourage the cat to come in through the flap rather than

to go out. To enhance the attraction of doing this, have some much-loved treats or favorite toys waiting for him just inside. Next, gradually lower the flap so that he has increasingly to push at it with head or paws to make it swing open.

This can take a considerable time with some kittens, but it will certainly work and usually within less than a week. Just be patient and never lose your temper during the learning process.

Going for a walk

Cats on leads

Although it's not as commonly seen as it is with dogs, cats, essentially highly independent creatures who love the freedom to move as they choose, can be trained to accept a lead and to go for walks on it.

Certain breeds are more amenable to lead-training than others. Persian types tend not to think much of it, but the Russian Blue in particular as well as many Siamese and Burmese cats will take to walking on a lead.

Early start

If you decide to lead-train your cat, begin early, while he is still very much a kitten. The lead must not be attached to the cat's collar but to a chest harness. Start by accustoming the kitten to the feel of the harness by putting it on him for short periods when he is indoors, but do not attach the lead or try to guide him anywhere with it at this stage. Don't rush him, as with all training patience is the prime virtue.

Once the kitten is totally unconcerned about wearing the harness and never tries to hook it off with a paw, you can attach a lead. Use one of the thin, light types that are designed for cats and toy dogs. Don't use the thick leather or thronged variety that is more suitable for hauling back a Mastiff.

Now let your cat move about the house, dragging the lead behind him. Take care that it doesn't get snagged on furniture or trodden on. Gradually extend the length of time the lead is attached.

When the cat is happy to tow his lead about all day, begin taking hold of it, first for short walks around the house, and then out into the garden in good weather. Avoid sharp tugs and never drag your cat. In time he will get the idea and come to enjoy your walks together. Do not persist if your cat is distressed by lead training or is frightened to be outside with no control over what happens to him.

Away from home

Walks away from home, down the street, or in the countryside are a different matter. The sudden appearance of a nosy dog or a strange cat can cause mayhem. Be ready, if necessary, to gather your cat up in your arms. Strolls in the park are usually practicable because you may well be able to take the cat's basket there with you and pop him into it as a refuge should something untoward occur. If your kitten is lucky enough to accompany you on a short break or holiday, you may find it useful to use a lead to help him explore his new, temporary home. You can keep control and prevent any bids for freedom in unfamiliar territory, especially when outside.

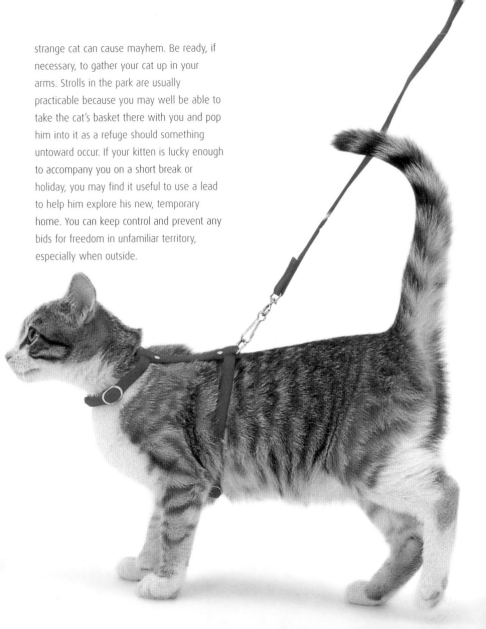

Stay, kitten, stay

Knowing when to stop

Sometimes it is necessary to halt your cat in his tracks to prevent him touching something, for instance a puddle of antifreeze liquid in the garage or the piece of fish you've just cooked for your supper.

This trick—I prefer to use the term behavior — is one of the easiest to teach your kitten. All you require, apart from the cat of course, is a quiet place with a table, a chair, and a good supply of food treat titbits. It is best to conduct the training sessions before mealtimes when the kitten is likely to be hungry.

Training sessions should last no more than four or five minutes, with two or three sessions a day. Eventually there will be no need to give a reward. The cat will respond to your spoken word alone.

You can now train another behavior, "sit," in the same way by putting the cat on the table, very gently pressing his hind end down if he doesn't sit automatically, saying the word "sssssit" with a soft "s" and then the cat's name and rewarding him in due course (see step 2 opposite).

TRAINING WITHOUT CRUELTY

Always remember that cats can only be trained with kindness, without any form of compulsion. Reinforce your kitten's good behavior with food treats and lots of praise.

1   Put the cat on the table and sit so that your heads are more or less on the same level. Do not stare directly into your kitten's eyes as this is seen as a challenge; blink slowly to put your kitten at ease. The cat will at first stand or sit, looking at you, and then he will lose interest, turn, and begin to move away.

2   Immediately say the cat's name, followed by "stay." Put your hand, palm open, in front of his face, about 12 in away. It is best to drawout the word "stay" to sound as "ssstay" with a soft "s"; cats respond to this sound. Be sure not to hiss though, as this sound could alarm your kitten.

3   If the cat stops promptly, say "good" followed by his name and offer a morsel of food or a treat as a reward. Repeat the process.

Come, kitten, come

You call, he comes . . . sometimes

Once your cat is obedient to the "stay" command, move on to "come." This is a valuable behavior that enables you to bring your cat indoors when necessary, but it also has a place in your relationship with a purely indoor cat.

Having become accustomed to the link between a command and a treat, your kitten will be keen to learn another variation of the procedure. This time there is no need for a table and chair, merely a quiet place and supply of treats.

Training sessions should last no more than five minutes, with two or three sessions a day. Watch your kitten's reactions to ensure the training remains fun. Bring every session to an end with lots of praise and fussing.

If your cat likes to go outside, it is a good idea to strengthen his response to the "come" command by letting him leave the house half an hour before his mealtime and then calling him in when his meal is ready. When he bounds in through the catflap or open door, be sure to have the food available at once and, of course, praise him fulsomely. If it isn't his mealtime why not do the same thing from time to time by calling him in for a tasty treat.

PATIENCE

On no account when you are training your cat let exasperation or ill-temper creep into your tone of voice. Never scold. Keep—and sound— happy and calm.

1 Put the cat on the floor, give the "stay" command in a quiet voice and then, when he is sitting or lying peacefully, back away from him to a distance of about 6 feet and stop.

2 Wait for a few seconds, then say in a cheerful tone of voice "come," followed by the cat's name.

3 If he complies satisfactorily, give the reward of a treat together with plenty of enthusiastic praise and petting. Repeat the process, but this time wait a little longer before giving the "come" command.

Begging to please

A most attractive behavior

Once your kitten has mastered "stay" and "sit," you can proceed to train him to do one of the most charming behaviors, to beg. Whenever thereafter you give treats for any reason, the "beg" position is the perfect, polite position for him to assume.

You can train any type of cat to do this, although the shorthaired breeds are the ones that generally become adept most quickly. You will be really delighted in future if your cat goes into the "beg" behavior without being cued, purely because he really is begging for a tasty treat.

Hold the training sessions in different locations around the house and also outside if the weather is good. Soon your cat will go into the "beg" position on command alone, although you shouldn't do that too often in case he begins to wonder what he's supposed to be begging for. Cats, you understand, insist on seeing the point of things.

Make sure that your cat is aware that you have some delicious treats close by, and then have him sitting by giving the "sit" and "stay" commands. Do be aware that teaching this trick could encourage your cat to beg every time there is food near. If this concerns you, try teaching the trick with a toy instead. A catnip toy is often the most effective.

TRAINING BY REWARD

Although cats are independent animals, many can be trained with the promise of tasty food treats. Always remember that the way your cat responds to training depends on his temperament.

1 Put some treats on a plate, or hold them in your hand, while the kitten watches and sniffs expectantly.

2 Raise the treats in front of and above the cat's head until it is just beyond the reach of his mouth with his neck fully extended. At the same time say "beg" together with his name. Be careful not to frustrate your kitten—if you sense any discomfort then stop training.

3 Sooner or later your cat will try to get at the treat with one or more paws. When he does so, say "good" followed by his name and give a treat. If he uses only one paw, lower the treats a little to encourage him to use both paws. Repeat the process several times but for no more than about five minutes, with two or three sessions every day.

Begging to please **111**

bad
behavior

Unwelcome calling cards

Misplaced marking

Cats use urine spraying and deposits of droppings as ways of marking territory. That's perfectly acceptable out of doors, even though your neighbors might find their lawn claimed in this manner, but why should your cat begin soiling indoors, even on your favorite chair?

Identifying the cause

It is often difficult to identify what triggers this type of behavior. In many cases it is the result of the cat feeling insecure or stressed for some reason. It can be the arrival of another pet or a new baby in the home or the cheeky entry of a neighborhood cat through the catflap. In multi-cat households, it may be related to competition between males and attempts to emphasize relative status. Essentially, it is so often all to do with territory.

Clearly, if you can identify the cause of the behavior you can take appropriate steps to improve things. Punishment of any kind must never be used, and it would, in any case, probably reinforce the cat's feelings of stress and anxiety.

Remedying the problem

Once a cat has deposited a scent in the home, he will be attracted to the same spot when the scent left there begins to fade and will do it again in order to refresh it. You should clean the marked location thoroughly. It is best to use first warm water and a detergent and then, when it is dry, to scrub the area diligently with disinfectant. Do not use cleaning liquids containing chlorine or ammonia because these chemicals occur naturally in cat urine, and using them could create confusion in the cat's mind.

When you've thoroughly cleaned the soiled area, you should reinforce the cat's sense of territory by repositioning his food bowls, favorite toys, and bedding around the soiled area. Another reassuring ploy is to wipe a piece of cloth across your cat's face to pick up some of his scent and then rub the cloth on places he has marked. This will help the cat to understand that this is his territory and he has no need to mark it again.

Soiling indoors

What's wrong with the litter tray?

Cats are essentially clean and fastidious animals. Nevertheless, they can sometimes urinate or defecate indoors, even when there is a litter tray at their disposal.

House training

Soiling indoors is not the result of the kitten having anxieties about his territory of the kind that leads to inappropriate marking (see pages 118–119). It can be because he is not fully house-trained or not yet competent in using the catflap to get outdoors. If there is no catflap, perhaps your cat lacks an efficient means of communicating to you that he needs letting out.

Some cats that normally go outside to relieve themselves may not be using a litter tray at all and—you will, of course, quickly spot this—lapse in their ways indoors only if it is, say, raining heavily or the local fighting tom is wandering around your garden.

Changing the tray

The problem often involves the litter tray itself. Like many humans, cats can be rather shy of relieving themselves in public view, and you should position the tray in a quiet, out-of-the way area in your home. Avoid a position by the catflap or in a hallway or under the stairs. Trays with hoods (see pages 94–95) give even more privacy and have the added advantage of reducing odor and the scattering of litter when the cat finishes his ablutions by raking with his feet.

Also like humans, cats don't like dining near the lavatory. They insist on keeping their gastronomic and toilet facilities well separated. If the food bowl and the litter tray are close to one another—I have seen such an arrangement very often—a cat may well refuse to do his business in the place you chose for him.

The actual type of litter can also be important. Cats like to relieve themselves on a soft substrate that is pleasurable to rake, and they find some types of wood pellet and

paper pellet litters rather unpleasant for their delicate foot pads to stand on and rake, particularly after being used a few times. They demonstrate their dislike of such litter by opting for a spot on your much softer carpet. Experiment with different forms of litter to find the type your cat prefers and is most comfortable with.

Inappropriate soiling

A checklist

Your cat may be soiling indoors because he is suffering from stress and feels that his territory is threatened or because his litter tray is wrongly placed and provided with the wrong kind of litter. If this is a problem for your cat, check with the points below so that you can take the appropriate action.

- Are you sure that this really is misbehavior and not some medical problem involving the bowel or urinary system needing veterinary attention? If you are in doubt, arrange for a veterinary examination of your cat.

- Can you identify anything that might be triggering soiling incidents (see page 117) and then deal with it appropriately?
- Is the soiling a reaction to some anxiety or stress outside or inside the home? Are there territorial disputes with neighbors'

cats that intrude, or among individuals in a multi-cat household? If you can identify a possible cause, try to eliminate or counter it. Do not punish your cat.

- Has anybody in the family upset the cat recently? Newly arrived adults, particularly people who are generally antipathetic towards cats, and young children sometimes disturb or alarm family pets.
- Has anything about the litter tray been changed recently (see pages 116–117)? Have you remembered to clean it on schedule? Have you changed the type of litter you've been buying?
- Have areas that the cat has previously soiled been properly cleaned and deodorized (see page 117)?
- If yours is a multi-cat household, do you have a litter tray for each pet? Cats generally prefer to have a "personal" litter tray for their sole use. Keep the trays in separate areas.
- Has the cat inadvertently been denied access to the litter tray or has the catflap jammed?
- Has your cat put on so much weight that he cannot easily pass through the entrance of a hooded litter tray? If a plump cat is having difficulty negotiating such an entrance, you will need to enlarge the doorway in the hood or invest in a bigger litter tray altogether. You should also, perhaps, consider enrolling your cat in a slimming program organized by your local veterinary clinic.

Starting from scratch

Your kitten's clawing the furniture

Cats frequently scratch in the house, usually in places they most definitely should not. It can be a way of marking their territory (see pages 74–75), but it is commonly also because they like the "feel," the texture, of the surface on which they are exercising and keeping their claws in shape.

If it's not the back of the sofa or an armchair, your cat is quite likely to choose embossed wallpaper as a scratching post.

Scratching posts

How can you stop this type of behavior? Scratching posts and pyramids or blocks of compressed corrugated paper, which you can find at the pet shop, will help. You can make a do-it-yourself version by wrapping a log in coarse sacking and, best of all, impregnating it with some catnip extract. Position the scratching posts in places where your kitten may feel vulnerable, for instance by doors or exits to the outside.

Your kitten has to be trained and encouraged to use such devices. As soon as you see the cat contemplating a scratching

CLAW COVERS

Some owners with valuable property put claw covers on their cats. These are available in the US, but they inhibit the cat from performing its perfectly natural scratching to mark his territory, and they can become contaminated when the cat covers faecal deposits.

session on a valued piece of furniture, grab hold of him and take him to the acceptable scratching location. When your kitten scratches in the correct place, give a reward signal, such as a clicker or bell sound, that your cat associates with a food treat (see pages 100–101) and then treat and praise your kitten. Start this type of teaching as early as possible. Multi-cat households will need more than one scratching device.

The surgical removal of the cat's claws under anasthetic by a vet is a rather extreme way of dealing with the scratching problem. This mutilation of an animal—and mutilation is what it is—is illegal in some countries, including Britain and Australia.

Over-grooming

Clean or too clean?

Cats enjoy being groomed, and they are often perfectly happy for you to do all the work. They also groom themselves, of course, and, in a multi-cat household, they groom other cats. However, grooming can become problem behavior when it is carried out to excess.

Out-of-control grooming

Grooming is an important feature of feline life, and it serves to keep the fur in good condition, reduces stress by stimulating the release of soothing endorphin chemicals within the body, and plays a part in cementing relationships with fellow cats and humans.

It becomes a problem when your kitten does virtually nothing else when he is not eating or sleeping. Large areas of hair may be removed by such incessant grooming. Baldness and skin inflammation may follow, and the cat becomes a rather unlovely sight. The ingestion of large amounts of hair, particularly by longhaired types, often leads to the formation of fur balls in the stomach. These accumulations may cause serious obstructions in the digestive tract that can necessitate surgery.

The causes and cures

If your cat does begin over-grooming, the first thing you must do is seek veterinary advice in case some kind of irritating skin disease is at the root of it.

If no skin disease is diagnosed, the cause is, again, likely to be stress and anxiety of some sort. It could be something like the arrival of another animal or a new baby in the house or a neighbor's noisy dog. If you can identify possible trigger factors, try to eliminate them.

If you suspect your kitten is over-grooming, take him to the vet. If necessary, the vet may refer your cat to a pet behaviorist.

Also, crucially, alter your cat's lifestyle to some degree to give him the opportunity of more peaceful time to himself. Put a snug bed for him inside, or on top of, a cupboard. And, of course, give him lots of frequent loving attention and fussing.

If your cat is a longhaired type, make sure that you groom him more frequently than usual to avoid the build-up of fur balls.

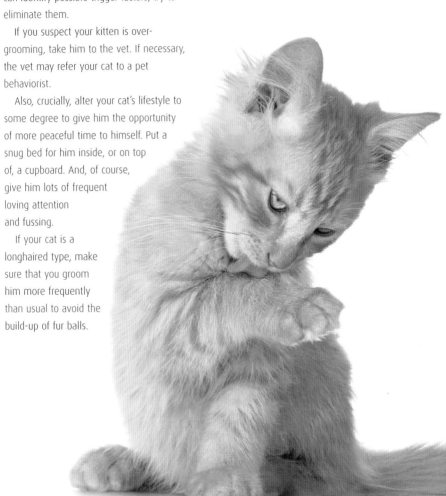

The perils of boredom

The home-alone cat

Although some pets seem to put up happily with eight or more hours to themselves, others do not, and then the devil finds work for the idle cat to do. It may come in the form of scratching or in-house soiling or in their attitude to you when you return.

Out all day

Your kitten can easily come to resent being left alone in the house if all the family are out at work all day. He may seem depressed, or he may be less active and playful than usual or eat and drink less. Alternatively, he may be far more demanding, pressing hard for attention, meowing non-stop, and, perhaps, howling indignantly.

How can you cope with this without going to the extreme of giving up your job? You should provide your kitten with lots of things, such as climbing frames, play stations, boxes, and cat toys of various kinds, to keep him amused. If it's practical, also think about bringing another cat into the family to solve the problem. Visit your local pet shop or search online to discover the range of toys

and activities that are now available. Some people leave a radio playing quietly all day, providing music or programs to suit their cats' preferences.

The psychological solution

You can also approach the problem psychologically. When you get home make sure you spend 15 minutes of playtime with your cat. Then for the next half hour have nothing to do with him. Ignore him. If he jumps on your lap, put him down on the floor without uttering a word. At the end of the half hour return to your normal behavior and interaction with him. It may take a week or even two of such training, with the cat almost pleading for your attention even more insistently, but eventually and without fail, he will come to understand that there are times when you can both have great fun together and times when you must each be free to do your own thing.

Strange appetites

Cats like the strangest things

Sometimes a cat will chew and, if allowed to, will swallow items that are definitely not suitable food for cats—or people. This sort of behavior can seriously harm your cat, and you must take steps to prevent it.

Eating habits

Among the odd things that cats eat are items made of plastic, rubber or paper, but the commonest bizarre "delicacy" is wool. Cats that fancy fabrics can be either purely chewers or purely eaters, whereas those that prefer paper may do both.

As you might expect, intestinal problems can result from the ingestion of these items, and wool is one of the most dangerous. Once wool-eating was thought to be practiced only by Siamese cats, but nowadays we know other types of Oriental as well as ordinary cats can do it. I once examined a Burmese cat that had swallowed a ball of wool. One end of the length of wool was still protruding from his mouth with the other trailing out of his back end.

Why it happens

Kittens can begin this unfortunate habit when they are not long weaned, and the commonest starting age is between two and four months. The reasons may include genetic factors, but that old enemy stress, particularly the stress of moving home as commonly happens to kittens, is often

the main cause. The frustration associated with boredom (see pages 124–125) is also often a contributing factor.

Tackling the problem

As ever, punishment must not be used. Obviously, denying the cat access to unsuitable material is desirable but often difficult in a cluttered household. There are a number of things you can do:

- Spray the targeted material with one of the safe deterrent aerosols obtainable from pet shops.
- Make your cat's normal mealtimes more interesting and fun: hide portions of food around your home, or try changing the kind of food you offer and include some that necessitates chewing.
- Provide a good selection of toys to encourage prey-attacking skills.

For advice on dealing with cats that eat houseplants see pages 128–129.

Cats as herbivores

Flower-fancying felines

Well fed though they might be, some cats seem to have horticultural aspirations and love to nibble plants both indoors and out. This can be beneficial, but be aware that some plants, found both indoors and out, are poisonous to cats.

Your cat may choose to nibble various plants because the leaves contain emetic chemicals that assist them in regurgitating fur balls, although it's just as likely that they simply like the texture. You can deter cats from chewing indoor plants by spraying them with a repellent aerosol, which you can buy in pet shops. Spraying plants outdoors is not always practicable, so take care, especially with young kittens, that they do not chew or lick poisonous plants (see pages 96–97).

Indoor gardening

Particularly if your cat has no access to a garden outside, provide him with a box in which you grow seedling grass. You can buy packets of specially prepared grass seed and the compost to grow it in in some pet shops. Other plants that they often relish and that you can safely grow for them are:

- Cereal grass (wheat or oats)
- Chickweed
- Colt's foot grass
- Nepeta (catnip)
- Sage
- Thyme

POISONOUS PLANTS

The following plants, both houseplants and those found growing outdoors, are poisonous. Do not allow your kitten access to them.

- *Caladium* (elephant's ears)
- Clematis
- *Dieffenbachia* (dumb cane)
- *Euphorbia pulcherrima* (poinsettia)
- *Hedera* (true ivy)
- Laburnum
- *Lathyrus odoratus* (sweet pea)
- Mistletoe
- *Nerium* (oleander)
- Philodendron
- *Prunus laurocerasus* (laurel, cherry laurel)
- Rhododendrons and azaleas
- *Solanum capiscastrum* (false Jerusalem cherry, winter cherry)

Fat cats

Overeating

Sometimes, and for some reason, cats begin to eat inordinate amounts, and, as you might expect, in most cases they put on weight. As with humans, obesity is becoming an increasing problem for cats.

Too much food

It is perfectly natural for cats to eat more than normal after giving birth or when they are recovering from a debilitating illness, but some cats do it when they are apparently in perfect health. It occurs more often in house-bound animals, and it can lead eventually to the development of serious diseases, including type-2 diabetes.

Reasons for overeating

Some overeaters are not in perfect health. Their gluttony can be due to a variety of conditions, such as parasitism, diabetes, pancreatic, and thyroid disease. The heaviest cat I know of was Spice, a ginger and white tom living in Connecticut. He weighed a mighty 43 lb, and this was due to an underactive thyroid gland. It is essential for all overeating cats to be examined by a vet without delay so that appropriate treatment can be provided if necessary.

The cause of the habit in otherwise healthy cats may be boredom, stress, or the way you feed your animals. Give the cat as much diversion as possible by playing with him often and supplying toys. If you can identify any source of stress in your cat's daily life (see pages 116–117 and 124–125), see if you can eliminate or, at least, diminish it. Restrict his food to meals fed twice a day, and remove the dish if the food is not polished off within 30 minutes.

Talk to your vet about the possibility of putting the cat onto a slimming diet using one of the proprietary cat-slimming, balanced foods now available and encourage exercise through play.

Leaving home

When a cat moves out

Much to your dismay, a cat can decide to pack his bags and leave home. Of course, you haven't been cruel to him in any way, you have fed him conscientiously, and you have been happy to see him curled up every night in his bed by the kitchen stove. So why has he gone?

No matter how tame, domesticated, and settled your kitten may seem to be, a cat remains independent of mind and will always be the decider and master of his own destiny. Among the reasons for his decision to go may be the following:

- He might have difficulties integrating with the neighborhood cats. This is not easy to solve, but you might be able to discuss matters with the neighbors who own the problem cat. If you are lucky, you might be able to agree on a timetable, governing the times at which your and their cats are allowed out.

- A new dog, cat, or human baby in the family can be upsetting. Make sure you give your cat plenty of attention and lots of play time.

- Your cat may wish to return to his old home if the family has moved house. Bring some of his bedding and possessions from the old house with you so that he

can identify with his own personal scent. Keep him strictly indoors for at least the first two weeks after arriving in your new home. Thereafter let him into the garden for a little exploration and exercise just before feeding time.

- Perhaps surprisingly, excessive interaction by owners can drive a cat away. Don't over-fuss your cat so that he comes more often to you looking for attention.

Shelter matters

Remember that your cat, which will bond far more strongly to his territory than to his owners, is likely to return home after venturing out of doors if he is adequately supplied with shelter from the elements, snug resting places that afford privacy, good food and, naturally, affection in his surroundings. This is much to be preferred to keeping a cat permanently indoors for fear of losing him.

Neutered? Not me

Still a lad about town

Does your neutered tom kitten remain keenly interested when a queen belonging to you or a neighbor comes into heat? It may be surprising, but it is not an uncommon occurrence.

Why should your neutered tom go through the full rigmarole of courting and mating with the female? Although the testicles are the main source of the male sex hormone, testosterone, other glands, the adrenals, also secrete tiny amounts, enough to make your castrated tom feel very macho, although, of course, there is no chance of him fathering any kittens.

Your neutered queen, even though she no longer comes in heat, might also become a source of great attraction to all the toms in the vicinity to such an extent that she feels harassed and becomes reluctant to go outside where she is likely to run into the toms. Again, the explanation for her continuing charms seems to be the scent of residual female chemicals, almost certainly hormones, that her body still produces.

There isn't much you can do for your queen if this occurs beyond making the garden or backyard as secure as possible against unwanted intrusions, by erecting

suitable trellis-work or netting on the walls or fencing. Ensure the trellis-work or netting is constructed at an appropriate height to keep out other cats. The only alternative is to keep her indoors permanently, although this should only be as a last resort.

Hypersexuality

Some cats can be over-sexed. In males this can, of course, be due to their not having been castrated or, curiously, according to some experts, where they have been deprived of so-called rapid eye movement (REM) sleep. It is believed that it is during the REM phases of sleep that cats, like humans, dream.

Hypersexuality in queens, manifested by prolonged and unusually frequent heat periods, is invariably a cystic condition of the ovaries. Speying, the operation of ovaro-hysterectomy, will cure the problem should it arise in your cat (see pages 80–81). Always seek advice from your vet on such matters.

Neutered? Not me **135**

Is your kitten crazy?

Mad moments

You know the sort of thing. One minute your cat is sound asleep on the rug, the next he springs to his feet and dashes furiously around, not going anywhere in particular, just going all out.

High spirits or illness?

This type of behavior is very amusing to watch, and the thud of his paws as he races up and down stairs can be surprisingly loud, even though he may still weigh only a few ounces. Some breeds, including longhairs and Birmans with big paws, sound distinctly heavy-footed.

Why should your beautiful bundle of fur suddenly explode in this way? You can normally put it down to sheer kittenish *joie de vivre*. However, strange behavior can be caused by brain disease of several types, among them infections (the most infamous one being rabies), tumors, poisons and hormonal disorders, but these are not, thank goodness, common.

Twitchy cat disease

One odd little phenomenon that you may come across is so-called twitchy cat disease. The kitten's skin suddenly begins to twitch and ripple, and then the cat jumps up and goes into the mad-dash routine, no destination especially in mind, that I have just described. He can sometimes appear to be hallucinating, as if he is frightened of something only he can see and was just

dreaming about. You will never know. Scientists think this behavior may be due to a brief alteration in the cat's brain chemistry that produces an effect similar to that of a human being on an LSD trip. The most important thing is that it is nothing for you to worry about. Your beloved kitten is not ill and most certainly not mad. He should settle down and return to normal before long.

Timid toms

Inborn feline fearfulness

There are several reasons for your kitten to become withdrawn and nervous, but in some cases, as with humans, timidity is something the cat has been born with.

Lots of kittens are bold, adventurous, extrovert characters. Others, by nature introverted and reserved, prefer most of the time to be hidden away under a bed or in a box in a secluded corner. They were born like this, and under no circumstances should such a kitten be punished or dragged out of his hideaway and forced to participate in the hurly-burly of everyday life. Compulsion and scolding have absolutely no place in his therapy. Be patient and gentle.

Alternative remedies

Many of these cats can be helped by alternative medicine techniques. Some vets offer homeopathic remedies, and they will prescribe anxiety-relieving preparations that are non-sedating, free of any side effects, and safe for all cats. Other products, in spray or room diffuser form, contain synthetic analogs of the natural calming pheromones found in a cat's facial glands. Used in the family home, they can reduce stress and anxiety in your kitten and may also be beneficial in combating other undesirable behavior, such as scratching and indoor spraying.

Don't rush

Whatever form of timidity is affecting his behavior—whether it is innate or acquired— you must let your kitten take his time and do

his own thing. When he does emerge to eat from time to time, do not rush at him enthusiastically. Don't be pushy. You must be patient and gentle, talking to him quietly in an encouraging way, petting him lightly, and giving him little food treats. It is often best if just one family member feeds him, at least to begin with, until he feels a little more confident with other people.

Who goes there?

Xenophobic cats

Many cats are suspicious of, or they actually and actively dislike, strangers, certainly for at least a short time after meeting them. This is hardly surprising given the somewhat fraught historical relationship between humans and cats.

Faulty socializing

The history of the domesticated cat's relationship with man over the millennia has been uneasy. Cats have frequently been maltreated or even persecuted, and the situation has improved only in relatively recent times, though even now cruelty is, sadly, not uncommon. So, there is in all cats, including our much-treasured family members, an instinctive wariness, which has been passed down from their forebears. This feline circumspection may be enhanced in some individuals by faulty socializing during kittenhood or an unpleasant experience at the hand of a human being later in life.

Your cat may demonstrate his fear of a stranger in various ways, perhaps appearing clearly distressed, vocalizing unhappily, or even attacking, if he imagines a threat and finds his escape route blocked. He may withdraw physically, shunning interaction and hiding, or he may withdraw emotionally, bottling up his fear and so risking the subsequent development of behavioral problems such as over-grooming. Your help in enabling your kitten to overcome his fears is of paramount importance.

As always, punishment is not an option. Gentle handling, praise, and treats are

important, but should not be overdone. Try to make the world around your cat more attractive and secure in feline terms. Be patient in coaxing him to interact with humans and organize "stranger training sessions" for him:

- Put your cat in a familiar cat basket some time before a "visitor," played by a family member whom the cat knows, enters. They should sit and talk to you but not approach the basket. Repeat this on at least six occasions, if possible daily.
- Next, do the same with a "real" visitor. Again, repeat the process several times.
- The "real" visitor should then enter the room when the cat is out of his basket and safe and calm in your arms. Repeat this several times.
- Finally, on each succeeding occasion, the "real" visitor should sit closer and closer to you both. Eventually the visitor should begin to stroke the cat gently.

All of this must be a very gradual process, and it may require many sessions over a period of weeks or even months until your cat feels confident with strangers.

Self-harming cats

Stop nibbling

It will understandably worry you if you notice that your kitten is incessantly nibbling and chewing away at some part of his body, often a paw, to the extent that he removes the fur and damages his skin, making it bleed.

Obviously, this sort of behavior might be due to irritation from some kind of skin disease, such as mange or ringworm, that requires veterinary attention, and you should seek professional advice at the first opportunity. However, some of these self-chewing cats are not suffering from any physical form of ailment. Rather, it's all in their minds.

Like over-grooming, self-mutilation, together with other phenomena such as obsessive self-licking and self-pawing, is stress related. Something in the cat's environment or the way he is treated is influencing his behavior.

As with other cat problems caused by anxiety and stress, you need to identify what has triggered his bizarre behavior. Then you can take steps to overcome or neutralize the triggers and find ways of more generally boosting the cat's confidence. You must provide opportunities for your cat to relieve his stress in other, non-damaging ways, such as being able to take refuge on some high-up shelf or another vantage point.

If no medical cause can be identified then your vet may refer your cat to a qualified professional. In some severe cases your vet might consider prescribing a form of tranquillizer as a short-term aid.

Night howlers

A little night music

There might be nights when you lie in bed listening to the caterwauling of cats on nearby rooftops. This type of nighttime carousing is not the sort of thing your well-brought-up, well-fed kitten, now curled up in his basket, would wish to take part in. Certainly not.

There is, however, another kind of cat music: howling by the family cat inside the house. This nocturnal yell is very distinctive and quite unlike the cat's other voices. It is sent forth more by older cats than young kittens, though young cats sometimes begin doing it when they are only a few months old.

Attention, please

So what is this all about? In a nutshell, it is a summons directed at you. Your cat is feeling a bit lonely and in need of reassurance. A common cause is the insecurity that follows some change in his environment, such as when he is alone or when, together with the rest of your family, he has moved home.

Unfortunately, the night yell habit persists long after whatever it was that triggered the anxiety originally has gone, and this is because your cat realizes that the yell always gets your attention. Once again, you have

with something resembling a faint smile beneath those whiskers. If you give in he'll do it again tomorrow night!

Silent nights

Although many owners would probably put up with this sort of behavior in an old, venerable individual, you should try to stop kittens indulging in it. You can, if you are resolute enough, harden your heart and ignore the summoning yell. Alternatively, you can try aversion therapy in the form of a squirt from a water pistol, or you could make a loud noise when the yell starts. You must be consistent, night after night, in using whichever approach you take. Sooner or later the yelling will stop—for good.

Of course, letting the cat sleep with you is another effective method and one that I suspect your kitten would heartily endorse, although not everyone will approve.

been trained! It's obvious: you jump out of bed as soon as you are sent for, go to the cat, talk to him, give him a stroke or two, and maybe pick him up. When you reach him, he's never writhing in pain or distress. No, he's sitting there, totally relaxed, and

Kitten gardener

Horticultural cats

Some cats have a passion for gardening. Unfortunately, they often practice their skills in your garden, the space on which you lavished time and effort and of which you are rightly proud.

Your cat might demonstrate his enthusiasm for gardening by digging up your cherished bulbs. This has nothing to do with his desire to cover up any droppings, unless, of course, the place where the bulbs are was previously one of his toilet areas. More often, it seems, he does it for sheer fun. He watches you plant them and decides to dig them up, apparently for the pleasure of watching you plant them all again. What a great game!

Stopping the fun

There are a number of ways you can bring your cat's fun to an end. Placing pieces of lemon peel or some cat-repellent granules, which are available from pet shops and some garden centres, around the bulbs is often very effective. You might also try spraying them with cat repellent aerosols.

Another excellent deterrent is to place wire mesh on the ground covering the bulbs. The plants will be able to grow through the mesh, but the cat will hate walking on it. If you are out in the garden when the kitten sets about his gardening activities, give him a quick squirt from a water bottle or turn on the lawn sprinkler, which can be a very effective signal of your disapproval and one that he will remember.

Don't forget to find some space in your herbaceous borders for a few valerian and nepeta plants that he can roll in to his heart's content. They should serve to deflect his attention from your other precious plants.

Fearful kittens

Coping with an agoraphobic cat

Although it's by no means a common phenomenon, you might just find yourself with a kitten that has a great fear of being in open spaces, whether indoors or outdoors. What happened to the self-reliant, confident, solitary hunter that we have talked about so much?

Causes of fear

If this odd feline agoraphobia manifests itself indoors, and your cat is highly reluctant to leave cover when it is in a room, it may be due to those early weeks of his kittenhood when he lacked the vital socializing training that should come from attention by his mother and human beings. Alternatively, there could have been, and perhaps still is, something outside the house that scares him: next door's barking dog, the pneumatic drilling of workmen on the road, or, yes, the unneutered tomcat that claims he owns all the gardens in the neighborhood.

Overcoming fear

You can help your cat get over this, of course, by keeping him permanently indoors, but if you've got a nice garden, why shouldn't the family kitten be able to use it?

The best solution is to erect in the garden an aviary-like, wire-mesh pen, which is closed on all sides, of the kind that breeders use for queens to rear their litters in. Construct plenty of safe hiding places in the pen. Put your kitten in the pen each day, at first for a short period, but gradually extending the length of time. Feed and play with him in there, so that he comes to regard the pen as a happy, safe haven. Eventually, the kitten can begin to go into the garden without being confined to the pen and you should keep an eye on him through a window to be sure that nothing bad happens.

It is ideal if there is a catflap that opens onto the garden so that if, at any time, your cat feels threatened he can dash indoors (see pages 102–103). Training your cat to walk on a lead (see pages 104–105) is another useful way of helping a timid cat lose his fear of the world around him and learn to love being outdoors.

Cat fights
Militant moments

It's hard to believe that your perfectly charming little kitten could ever get involved in anything as vulgar as a fight. Sadly, however, differences of opinion arise in the best regulated households, and you need to know how to rescue your kitten when the time comes.

Territorial disputes

Cats don't go looking for trouble. They prefer to avoid confrontation and, wisely, have developed communication systems (see pages 62–63) that inform other cats of their intentions and their desire, usually, to steer clear of an altercation.

When scraps do occur they are frequently about territory, particularly where local neighborhood cats are involved. It can become a widespread problem involving a large number of animals and, inevitably, their owners are often dragged into it, with subsequent ill feeling possibly developing between the humans.

Dealing with intruders

If you and your cat find yourselves in such a position, it may not be enough merely to use deterrent measures against outsider cats that intrude into your garden or actually come into your house through the catflap. Certainly there is a place for such things as squirts from a water pistol directed at invaders. They soon learn. However, cats are intelligent and they know not to make their illicit incursions until you are out of the house. Booby traps in the form of water sprays or noise-makers activated when the householder is not present are more effective. Take care not to hurt the intruder though.

Neighborhood watch

Sometimes the feline wars around your home reach the point where they call for the cooperation of a group of neighbors. Ideally, all cat owners appreciate the importance of making their pet's home a snug and secure base in which he is well treated and cared for and to which he loves to return. Initially, it might be possible for one neighbor's cat to be kept in at a time when another cat is out and about and vice versa. Such arrangements do work if the people involved show the goodwill they would like their cats to display toward their fellow creatures.

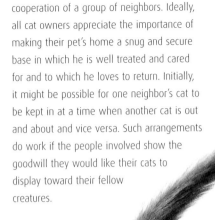

Family feuds

Outbreaks of in-house aggression

Cats are not out for trouble and generally prefer a quiet life. However, in a multi-cat home spats between cats are not uncommon. Even cats that have lived amicably together for many years can, out of the blue, turn on each other, and when a new kitten joins the family there is increased potential for trouble.

Pressures on space

Conflict is more likely to arise where a considerable number of cats live in a small house, so that there is competition for hideaways, high-up resting places and limited supplies of food or owner attention. One or more of the pets may also have been deprived of socialization training by his

mother or human owner during kittenhood. The latter is the commonest factor.

The make-up of your home's cat family plays a big role in determining how peaceable life is likely to be. Genetic factors are important: some cats are innately more tolerant of living in restricted territory, and others are not. Generally, you will find that the most harmonious multi-cat households are composed of littermates.

Absence and reintroduction

Trouble between family cats can also erupt if one of them is away for a matter of days—at the vet's for an operation, in a cattery for some reason, or just straying. When he returns, he may be received as a stranger.

We discussed the introduction of new pets into a household on pages 30–31, and you can use the methods suggested there to re-integrate a cat that has been temporarily elsewhere. Alternating the use of feeding bowls, bedding and toys between the various cats will also help in the process.

Make sure that there are sufficient refuges, resting places, high vantage points, and escape routes for all your cats. Give each cat his own food bowl, and don't let them think you have a favorite. Spread your attention equally among them.

Evasive action

If a spat does erupt be careful about intervening. Trying to separate the contestants in the manner of a boxing referee can be counterproductive and might actually increase the tension level. Your best plan is to aim to distract them with food tidbits and toys they can chase. Never attempt to strike them.

Squabbling cats

A checklist

The introduction of a new kitten into a household in which there is already one or more established cats can lead to problems. The established cats will feel jealous if you lavish too much attention on the newcomer, and the additional pressure on the available spaces within the home can lead to tension that eventually erupts into fights.

- Is it male-on-male quarrelling? Have the cats involved been castrated? Unneutered toms are more likely to squabble and fight. Get your male cats neutered.
- Is some factor causing fear and anxiety in your cat? Can you identify and eliminate the problem?
- Has your cat got plenty of refuge places, particularly ones high up, and escape routes always available when he needs to avoid confrontation?
- Is your cat involved in territorial skirmishes outside?
- If your household is a multi-cat one, does each cat have some space it can call his own?
- Have you recently introduced a new cat or kitten into your house (see pages 30–31)?

- In a multi-cat home, do your pets have to compete for bowls at feeding time or for your attention?
- Are you even-handed in showing affection to all your cats?

- Don't pet the cat on your lap for too long on any one occasion to avoid getting bitten (see pages 68–69).
- If one of the cats in a multi-cat house is elderly, he may be suffering from a condition such as arthritis, overactive thyroid gland, or certain tumors that are giving him pain and causing him to be tetchy. If you suspect this is the cause, book a visit to the vet.

you, the carer

Every little thing

Equipping your home for a kitten

You undoubtedly want your new kitten to feel that he has landed, if not in luxury, then at least, in a place of comfort and security. Consider carefully what you buy for him.

Carrying basket

The first item you will have to buy so that you can safely collect your new kitten from his original home is a carrying basket or

container. The traditional type is a basketwork, kennel-like construction with a door, often of metal mesh, hinged at one side. The problem with this sort of carrier is that a determined cat can sometimes push the door away from the basketwork frame and get out. They are, in addition, drafty and not easy to clean.

Far better are the hard vinyl, fiberglass, or polyethylene carriers, which are not only escape-proof but are also easy to clean.

For a one-off, out-of-the-blue carrier—say to the vets or cattery in an emergency—a disposable, strong cardboard carrier, generally obtainable from animal charities and some pet shops, can be used.

No matter what type of container you obtain for your cat, make sure that it is big enough for the cat in question, well-ventilated, and easy to carry, clean, and disinfect after use. If it is only for a short journey, it is generally not necessary to furnish the container with food and water.

Litter tray

A litter tray is essential, even if your new kitten will normally be expected to go outside to relieve himself. Come the day he feels a bit off-color or it is raining heavily, he may not be so inclined. It is best to have more than one litter tray in a multi-cat household, ideally one for each cat, but certainly more than one. Some cats are fussy about sharing facilities, and no one likes to be kept waiting long. Don't forget to buy a scoop so that you can remove the litter every day.

Bed

An important item of feline furniture is the cat bed. These come in a wide range of designs, including hammocks to hang over radiators. Pick one that is big enough for your curled-up cat. You will need to provide some soft, snug lining, such as a cushion or, best of all, a piece of sheepskin. Thinly coated types of cat, such as the Rex, relish the provision of an electric heating pad and such a device is particularly comforting for very young kittens who have recently left the warmth of their mother's body.

Feeding bowls

Food and water bowls for the sole use of the kitten should be solid enough not to be readily flipped over, and easy to clean. In a multi-cat household each cat must have his own bowls.

Kitting out kitty

Essential items for your kitten

Apart from the basics of eating, sleeping, and pottying, a loving owner will provide other items for his new kitten. Pet shops and online suppliers stock an amazing range of items and offer plentiful ways for you to spend large amounts of money.

Catflap

If you expect your new kitten to use the garden to relieve himself, a catflap fitted into a door or wall will be an essential item, not an optional extra so that that you will have no need to act as doorman to your pet's exits and entrances.

Most catflaps have catches that can be adjusted to permit the cat's passage in one or both directions and some can be opened only by your cat if he is carrying a small magnetic device on his collar. This system is ideal for preventing the entrance of foreign neighborhood cats, especially bold unneutered toms.

Collar

You may or may not decide to get a collar for your kitten, particularly if he is microchipped (see page 185). Collars with name tags do help neighbors, who, naturally enough, don't possess microchip readers to identify your cat.

All collars must have a built-in elastic insert to allow the cat to escape if it gets snagged on a tree branch. If you are planning to train your kitten to walk on a lead then you will also need a harness (see pages 104–105).

Scratching posts

Prevention being better than cure, you may well save your furniture from being mauled by your kitten by providing a scratching post, pad, or pyramid.

In-house entertainment

Cats that live entirely indoors can suffer from boredom, leading to them becoming sluggish or perhaps getting up to mischief. A scratching post will give him something to do, but it is even better if you can install one or more of the climbing frames or play stations that are especially designed for cats and that you will find online or in one of the larger pet shops.

Toys for your new kitten are essential, and you will find a wide variety on the market. Just as much fun for cats as purchased toys, however, are household items, like cardboard boxes, which can be endlessly explored, and old ping-pong balls.

Take care with items that have lengths of string attached. They will fascinate your kitten but may result in dangerous entanglement. Don't leave such toys lying around when no one is there to keep an eye on him and play with him.

Grooming equipment

Finally, don't forget to buy some grooming equipment. You will need a fine-toothed comb, a soft brush, a hard brush, a hand glove brush, chamois leather, cotton wool, and pieces of soft cloth. You might also need some claw clippers, which your vet will be able to supply and show you how to use.

Signs of trouble

Is your kitten unwell?

It is good practice for you to inspect your cat at least once a week (see pages 56–57). You may then detect the first signs of potential problems, particularly concerning his eyes, ears, nose, and skin. However, as with human infants, ailments can, and often do, strike out of the blue.

What to watch out for

Among the signs that something is amiss with your kitten are:

- General listlessness and an unusual amount of vocalizing, which might indicate pain, though be aware that with some painful conditions your cat may be more silent than usual.
- Coughing, panting, shallow breathing, wheezing, and sneezing.
- Excessive eating, excessive thirst, loss of appetite, bad breath, constipation, and diarrhea. Soiling in the house may not be misbehavior but due to bowel or kidney and bladder upsets.
- Limping, unsteady gait or weakness of the legs, walking with the head tilted to one side, or a tendency to move in circles.
- Irritation of the skin, excessive biting or licking or pawing at areas of the skin.
- Abnormal appearance of one or both eyes, including cloudiness or bloodshot.

If you do happen to find your kitten is suffering from any of the signs listed above, don't delay. The condition of a young kitten in particular can worsen rapidly. Seek veterinary advice immediately.

PAINFUL PURR

It has been known that as well as purring when happy, cats can purr when they are injured or frightened, as a stress reliever. It is also believed that purring can encourage healing.

Taking your cat's pulse

Your cat's pulse can be felt best in the groin on the inside of a thigh. Place two fingers on the inside of one of his thighs. The pulse should be strong and regular with a rate of 110–140 beats per minute.

On the sick list

Dealing with an ill cat

There are a number of illnesses and problems that can arise suddenly.
When you get to know your kitten well, you will be able to judge
whether he is suffering from nothing more than an upset stomach
from overeating or whether it is something more serious. If you have
any doubts, contact your vet immediately.

Vomiting

If your cat is vomiting check that he has not
been in an accident. Does he seem dull and
depressed? If he has dilated pupils after
eating within the last half hour it could be
serious. One of the most serious diseases of
cats is feline infectious enteritis, also known
as feline panleucopenia, which is caused by
a virus. This is, fortunately, a complaint
against which your cat may well have been,
or is due to be, vaccinated (see page 170).

Non–serious causes of vomiting include
overeating, ingesting the feathers of a wild
bird that he has caught, over-excitement,
dietary upsets, and, particularly in longhaired
types, fur balls.

Diarrhea

If there is blood in the diarrhea, if the cat is
also vomiting or if it is dull and depressed it
could be serious and the result of feline
enteritis or poisoning. Less serious causes are
milk intolerance (some cats cannot digest
cow's milk), worms, and mild infections.

Overeating or excessive thirst

Overeating can be the result of parasites or
glandular or pancreatic disorders. Consult
your vet if your kitten overeats for more than
two weeks. If, at the same time, he is also
drinking excessively, this could indicate
diabetes. Seek veterinary attention at once.

Excessive thirst, which is commonly
associated with diabetes, can also be a sign
of kidney, liver, or hormonal diseases.
Diabetes does occur in kittens but is much
commoner in older, overweight cats and
cases are on the increase.

Unusual breathing patterns

If your cat is under one year old and is
breathing heavily or rapidly and also has

diarrhea, is vomiting or has dilated pupils, perhaps with a discharge from his eyes and/or nose, or if his breathing is very slow and fails to improve when disturbed, this could be serious. Possible causes include poisoning, feline influenza, and feline leukemia. The two latter diseases are of viral origin, and all kittens should be vaccinated against them. Seek immediate help from your vet.

More possible problems

Identifying illnesses

Most cats that are well cared for, well fed, and stress-free rarely fall ill, but in addition to the general symptoms described on pages 164–165, your regular inspections of your cat might reveal evidence of other maladies.

Leukemia

Feline leukemia attacks a kitten's immune system, making him susceptible to other ailments. Usually, by the time they are eight months old, kittens are resistant to this infection and there is thus an argument for keeping your cat indoors until it is that age.

Feline infectious peritonitis

This is a particularly serious disease and is a risk especially where there is a large group of cats, as at a cattery. When they reach about three years of age cats are, in most cases, naturally immune to it.

Mouths

Mouth troubles in cats are quite common, and you should pick up the signs early on with your weekly health check-ups. Cats don't normally have bad breath unless they've just eaten some fish, and an unpleasant odor, often accompanied by drooling of saliva, invariably means mouth infection, bad teeth, or tongue ulcers. Arrange a visit to the vet.

Eyes

There are several possible medical conditions of the cat's eyes, although blindness is quite rare. They include bulging of the eye, partial covering of both eyes by the third eyelid (the white membrane that is hidden in the corner of the eye between the eyeball and the lid), painful eyes, and discharges. Painful eyes with excess tear production can be the result of foreign bodies, often grass awns. Whatever the symptoms, seek immediate veterinary advice for any eye problem.

Ears

If you do not make sure that your kitten's ears are clean at all times, they may be invaded by one or more of a number of undesirable items. Is your cat shaking his head? Is there a sticky discharge from the ear? Ear inflammation can be caused by an invasion of ear mites or by infection with bacteria or fungi, and not infrequently all three are present at the same time. Your vet

will recommend the appropriate medication, usually in the form of drops or creams.

A staggering gait, a tendency to tilt the head to one side, or walking in circles often indicate the presence of infection in the cat's middle ear, beyond the eardrum. This condition calls for immediate professional treatment, principally through antibiotics.

Looking after your kitten

Nursing an ill cat

If your kitten is ill you must be able to handle him so that you cause him no additional distress or pain, and your vet will prescribe medication that you will have to administer yourself.

Handling an ill cat

So that you can attend to a sick cat needing examination or medication you will have to handle him. There are four ways of doing this:

- If your cat is not in pain the best and most gentle way is to cradle him in your arms, holding him close to your body.
- You can hold your cat by the scruff of his neck and press him down firmly on a table or other flat surface. In this position he cannot easily bring his claws into play and scratch you.
- Place your cat on a flat surface so that he is lying on his side and hold all four limbs firmly, both forelegs together in one hand, both hindlegs in the other.
- Wrap the cat in a large towel, blanket, or sack and hold him close to you cradled in you arms. For added security, grasp the scruff with one hand through the material.

TASTY MEDICINE

These days many cat medicines are available in a palatable form that a cat will happily consume in his food or even straight from your fingers. Your vet will advise you on the best way to administer the medication being prescribed for your kitten.

Administering medicines

When you have to administer medicines to your kitten, do as follows:

1 Put your cat on a flat surface and take hold of his head with one hand as if it were a ball.

2 Bend his head back gently. His mouth will then open automatically and you can use your index finger and thumb to push the lips on each side in between the cheek teeth. If you are giving your cat a tablet, drop it accurately onto the groove at the back of the tongue and give it a quick poke with the index finger of your free hand or a teaspoon handle.

3 If the medication is in liquid form drip it very slowly into the cat's open mouth. It must be drop by drop, giving the cat the chance to swallow. Close his mouth immediately and gently stroke down the throat with a finger of your free hand: this will encourage the cat's swallowing reflexes.

Protecting your kitten

Vaccinations

It is essential that your kitten is vaccinated as early as possible
against some of the most dangerous virus diseases that can affect
cats. You must take care that your kitten doesn't pick up a virus from
neighborhood cats until he is immune, and you should keep him
away from possible sources of infection, best of all confining him
indoors, for two weeks after his first dose of vaccine.

Viruses

The viruses against which cats are vaccinated
are the two kinds that cause cat flu, feline
panleucopenia virus, the cause of feline

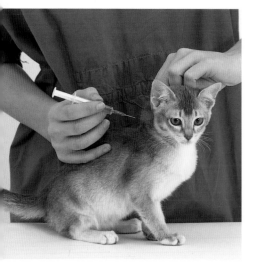

enteritis, and feline leukemia virus. If you live
in certain parts of the world your cat can be
vaccinated against the rabies virus. In some
countries a vaccine against feline infectious
peritonitis is now available, but as yet there
is no available protection against the non-
viral feline infectious anemia.

Vaccination can be carried out only on
healthy animals. Although there have been
some reports of nasty reactions at the
injection site of some feline leukemia
vaccines, in the vast majority of cases
immunization is trouble-free and without side
effects. Very occasionally transient local or
more generalized reactions do occur with any
vaccine, but they are easily dealt with.
Vaccination cannot, of course, give protection
to an animal that is already incubating the
disease, nor is it a treatment. Always keep
your cat inside until he has been vaccinated.

Timing

Discuss with your vet when will be the appropriate time to take your kitten for vaccination. In most cases the "starter" vaccination course consists of two injections, three to four weeks apart, with the first one administered at eight to nine weeks of age. After that your cat will require a single booster dose of vaccine once a year.

Cats can be vaccinated separately for each of the diseases mentioned above and, where used, rabies vaccine is always a separate shot. Nowadays, however, three-in-one vaccines that protect against cat flu, enteritis, and leukemia in a single injection are most commonly used.

Certificates

You will receive a vaccination certificate from the vet. Keep this safe to remind you when your kitten needs his annual booster, and take it with you to the vet when the time comes. Most importantly, if ever your cat goes into a cattery, you will have to show the up-to-date certificate before he will be accepted for boarding.

Internal parasites

Keeping your kitten worm free

The parasites that can invade your kitten are of two main kinds: those that live inside and those that live outside his body. The ones commonly living inside the cat include various kinds of worms.

Problem worms

Of the parasitic worms that sometimes affect cats the most important are the ones that make their homes in the intestinal tract and often, as larval forms, in other organs. They include roundworms, tapeworms, whipworms, threadworms, hookworms, and flukes.

Some adult worms, such as hookworms and whipworms, are bloodsuckers. Tapeworms don't suck blood: they simply steal some of the cat's food. Larval roundworms can infest fetal kittens while they are in the womb and may also be present in the mother's milk. Once inside a kitten, these larvae migrate through the liver, heart, and lungs to reach the intestine, causing much damage and discomfort to the kitten on the way. This is why kittens are more seriously affected than adults and may be in poor condition, anemic and pot-bellied, as well as suffering from diarrhea or constipation.

Tapeworms don't normally produce symptoms in the cat beyond flatulence and irritation when parasite segments pass through the anus. Frequently, the only sign you will detect of tapeworms is seeing one or two of these segments, looking like grains of boiled rice, stuck to the fur of your kitten's rear end. If you suspect your kitten has worms, take him to the vet immediately.

Problem protozoans

Another kind of internal cat parasite is a tiny protozoan that, like the malaria parasite of human beings, lives inside red blood cells. Although sometimes present in only small numbers and not causing any symptoms, when large numbers invade the cat's blood, destroying red cells, they cause the disease feline infectious anemia. If uncomplicated, this condition can be successfully treated by the vet. Sometimes, however, it occurs along with feline leukemia and the prognosis is then much more grave.

Preventive measures

You can keep your kitten parasite free by following preventive measures, including:

- Give regular anti-worm medication, obtainable from your vet or pet shop, throughout your cat's life.
- Prevent your cat from eating wildlife which carry the parasites in some form.
- Groom your cat regularly and use anti-flea preparations because fleas carry worm larvae.
- Change and wash your cat's bedding regularly to clean out any skin-burrowing worms lurking there.
- Dispose of litter in a hygienic way by burning, burial, or throwing it in the dustbin.

External parasites

Keeping your kitten flea-free

As well as internal parasites, cats can be troubled by a range of parasites that live on the outside.

Insect pests

The commonest skin parasite of the cat is the flea, which can be of the feline, dog, or human variety. The attentions of these tiny bloodsucking nuisances make the cat scratch, twitch, and lick himself in irritation. If you look closely into your cat's fur you might not be able to spot any of the ever-elusive insects themselves, but their presence is clearly betrayed by what looks like coal dust in the coat. These are flea droppings.

Two kinds of louse—suckers and biters—can also infest cats, and although they may attach themselves anywhere on your kitten's body, their favorite place is the head.

If you live in the country your cat might pick up sheep ticks when he is out patrolling the fields. These creatures are bloodsuckers, and they swell up to resemble blackcurrants when they are full of kitten blood.

In autumn, outbreaks of irritating dermatitis are sometimes caused by harvest mites, while fur mites can cause cat dandruff. Various species of mites like to burrow into cat skin and produce mange, a chronic skin inflammation. The most commonly affected areas are the head and ears.

Keeping control

Watch, particularly while doing your weekly checkups (see pages 56–57), for any signs in your cat's coat of baldness or inflammation. If you find anything amiss, seek professional advice or, if you are sure you know the cause, use some form of medication in the form of anti-parasitic powders and systemically acting pour-on drops.

Fleas lay their eggs on the cat without cementing them to hairs as lice do, so there is a strong probability that flea eggs are lying incubating in your house, on carpets and furniture and, especially, in the cat's bed. Use special aerosols to treat your cat's living areas to stop the eggs from hatching.

Do not pull sheep ticks off your cat's skin because the ticks' mouthparts are buried in the skin, and if these are left behind they can form abscesses.

Ringworm

Ringworm is a fungal skin parasite. It causes various kinds of lesion on the skin. If you suspect ringworm ask your vet to confirm the diagnosis and then provide the appropriate treatment of oral anti-fungal medicines and skin lotions.

Holiday? What holiday?

Staying in a cattery

If you have to put your kitten in a cattery while you are away on holiday you need to be certain that you choose somewhere where he will be well looked after and be kept safe from illness and accidents.

Finding a cattery

The first step in finding the best possible cattery for your cat is to ask cat-owning friends or breeders. Your veterinary clinic may also be able to recommend somewhere suitable that is within a reasonable traveling distance and has a good reputation.

Next, pay an inspection visit and investigate the following:

- Are the boarded pets kept in separate accommodation, with no possibility of direct contact with other animals?
- Are there both snug, draft-free, indoor sleeping quarters as well as a reasonably

spacious, escape-proof outdoor run equipped with furniture that your cat will enjoying climbing on and playing with?

- If the cattery is essentially a building containing rows of cages, the cage sides that are made of mesh should be set into the exterior walls of the building. Cage sides inside the building should be solid; none of them should be made of mesh. This design feature is important chiefly because it avoids the circulation of air among the cats within the building; instead they breathe fresh air from outside, reducing the risk of virus spread.

- What are the feeding arrangements? Can you bring your kitten's favorite food or do they have it among the many varieties that the cattery already stocks?

- What is the cattery's procedure if a cat falls ill? Who is their vet? Does he visit to make routine checks and, if so, how often? If a cat falls ill, is there a quarantine or hospital room available if the vet considers it necessary? Make sure you leave contact telephone numbers, including that of your vet, if you decide to board your kitten here.

- Must all cats coming to be boarded have been vaccinated against feline enteritis and feline influenza? If this is not the case, this is not the cattery for you or for your

STAYING AT HOME

Many cat owners prefer to leave their cats at home and to ask a friend or neighbor to pop in regularly to put down fresh food, wash the bowls and dishes, and, if necessary, change the litter tray. If you are out at work all day, your cat may be used to being alone, and he will probably be happier at home. However, if you live near a busy road or if you do not know someone reliable, you will have to find a cattery.

kitten. A reputable cattery will insist that owners bring valid vaccination certificates when they are boarding a cat. This is essential. Verbal assurances are not sufficient.

- If you are bringing more than one cat from your multi-cat family to be boarded, can they be kept together, assuming, of course, that they already get along well with one another? This is not absolutely essential, but it is preferable.

- Are the premises clean and in good condition overall? Do the staff seem efficient and caring?

Feline first aid

Accidents happen

Cats do seem to have fewer accidents than dogs, probably because they have bodies that are lighter and more lithe, and they are more agile in avoiding trouble. However, if your kitten's luck does one day run out, here are a few suggestions as to how to deal with some of the commoner forms of feline accident before you take him to the vet.

Road accidents

Move the cat out of danger by slipping a sheet under him as a hammock. Take him to a quiet, warm place and lay him down on his side. Cover him with a blanket and put a covered hot water bottle (not too hot) next to him. Make sure that his mouth is clear of blood or vomit and pull his tongue forwards. Remove his collar if he is wearing one. Staunch any heavy bleeding with pads of gauze or cotton wool. Call the vet.

Drowning

Firmly grasp both hindlegs together in one hand and whirl the animal around at arm's length. It may look brutal, but this is the best way of forcing water from the cat's lungs by centrifugal force. Call the vet.

Burns

The commonest type of cat burn is caused by hot liquid. Apply ice or cold water to the affected area as quickly as possible and then anoint it with a greasy ointment, such as Vaseline or petroleum jelly.

In summer the ears of white cats sometimes get sunburned. Ask your vet for some anti-inflammatory ointment to treat affected ears. Prevent it happening again by keeping the cat indoors on sunny days or work a little human suntan cream into the ear flap before your cat goes outside.

Poisoning

If you suspect that a cat that is vomiting, having convulsions, or is comatose may have been poisoned then call your vet. He will treat the animal once he has diagnosed the probable nature of the poison. Meanwhile, wash the cat in case the toxic substance is on his coat and is being absorbed directly through the skin or he may licked it. Use human baby shampoo, rinse, and then dry your cat thoroughly. If possible, take a sample of any suspected poison to the vet together with the cat.

quick
reference

Things to do before your kitten arrives

First steps

If you have not already selected your new kitten, your action plan must begin with deciding what type of cat you want. Then you must check that you have everything that your new kitten needs for his comfortable, pampered life.

Pedigree or crossbreed?

Unless you intend to show and probably breed from your cat later on, crossbred animals make just as delightful, interesting, and attractive pets—sometimes more so—than expensive pedigrees. Cat rescue homes and cat charities will have dozens of kittens that you will instantly fall in love with.

If you do pay a visit to one of these admirable establishments you may, of course, see older cats needing a good home. Such individuals may have had tough lives so far, be set in their ways, and be slower to adapt to a new environment, but they will probably be house-trained and less demanding than a young kitten, which will need to be house-trained. Even crusty old cats with bad experiences of people will respond eventually if you patiently give them love and attention.

Male or female?

Both sexes of cat make equally good pets, but unless you want to breed in the future, they should be neutered (see pages 80–81).

One kitten or two?

If you have enough room in your home for all their equipment and paraphernalia, and particularly if no one is in the house during the day, two kittens would keep each other occupied. A kitten alone can suffer from boredom, which can lead to problem behavior (see pages 124–125).

Is your house suitable?

What modifications, if any, will you have to make in your house?

- Is the garden secure to prevent escapes?
- Do you have a garden pond that will need a cover?

- Will you have to have a catflap installed?
- Are there young children or pets in the household who might react badly to the kitten's arrival (see pages 30–31)?

What equipment do you need?

Have you got all the necessary paraphernalia to care for your new kitten, including a carrier, a litter tray and litter, a bed, suitable food, and some toys (see pages 160–161)?

When you collect your cat

Only when you are certain that everything at home is ready for the new arrival can you go to collect him (see pages 28–29). Before you bring him home, however, check that:

- You have the available information on the past health and any vaccination history of the kitten. Is a vaccination certificate available? What diseases does it cover?
- You know what he has been fed on. Can you take a sample home with you when you collect him?
- You can take him to a vet to check him over before you take him home.
- You have someone to accompany you—an adult or an older child—when you go to collect him (see page 28).

Things to do now your kitten is safely home

Don't panic

Introducing your new kitten into your house can be a stressful time for everyone concerned. There are several things you can do to make this a pleasant and enjoyable time for you and for your kitten.

Checklist

- Introduce your kitten into his strange new house and show him around (see pages 30–31 and 36–37).
- Keep your kitten indoors for the first two or three days (see pages 30–31).
- Make sure you have some suitable cat food in the house, although ideally you will have asked the breeder to give you a small amount of the food your kitten has become used to when he was weaned.
- Make introductions to the rest of the human and pet family (see pages 30–33).
- Begin toilet training at once (see pages 94–95).
- When he is ready, let him out into the garden for the first time (see pages 96–97).

- Begin name training at once (see pages 98–99).
- Have your kitten microchipped (see below).

Microchipping

Have your kitten microchipped by the vet for identification purposes in the future, in case he gets lost or you decide to take him abroad and have to pass through customs. Some countries that issue so-called pet passports for animals that have to be moved across borders insist on the use of microchips.

The microchip is a tiny electronic gadget about the size of a grain of rice that is injected under your cat's skin and stays there permanently. It carries within it a registration number that is specific to your cat alone, and the number can be read by holding a chip-reading device close to the cat. Most vets and many cat charities, police, and border-post personnel possess these readers. You will be given a record of the number, which you should keep in a safe place, and the number will be on the registers of organizations that specialize in tracing lost pets. Your vet will advise you on how to contact them.

Things to do now your kitten is safely home

Things to do in the future

Long-term plans

As your kitten settles into his new home and begins to show his own personality, you can begin to develop a lasting and rewarding relationship with him and to take steps for his long-term welfare. The first weeks are the most important.

Checklist

- Make sure your kitten is vaccinated against important viral diseases when he is eight to nine weeks old. A second dose is usually given three to four weeks later, and thereafter he will need annual booster vaccinations.
- Have your cat neutered. A female should be at least three months old, a male nine months old (see pages 80–81).
- Groom your cat regularly (see pages 46–47).
- Inspect your cat once a week to spot any developing health problems early (see pages 56–57).
- Make sure you accustom your cat to traveling in your car (see pages 42–43).

Training

Begin training your kitten with two or three sessions a day if you have the time. Train one behavior at a time and move on to another only when your cat has mastered it. Once trained, keep refreshing his abilities by regular "performance" sessions.

- Stay (see pages 106–107)
- Sit (see pages 106–107)
- Come (see pages 108–109)
- Beg (see pages 110–111)

If the cat is on your lap and kneading you, and has a tendency to keep his claws out, train him to be a gentle cat (see pages 68–69).

Pregnancy

If, by accident or your design in having her mated, a female becomes pregnant, she will deliver her kittens on average 65 days after conception. Kittens born earlier than 58 days are usually born dead or very feeble while those born later than 71 days are bigger than normal and also often dead. If you suspect your cat is pregnant, consult your vet.

Once you see your queen is pregnant you must make preparations for the birth (usually births) by constructing a "maternity ward" in the form of a kittening box of wood or cardboard, lined with sheets or, better, newspaper, that you can put in a quiet, out-of-the-way place. Introduce the queen to it well before she kittens, if possible. If she elects to give birth in a different spot, take the box to her.

Index

Acknowledgments

Many, many thanks to Trevor Davies, Kerenza Swift, Charles Hallam, and all the rest of the superb editorial team at Hamlyn. And to my five Birman cats who, draped over the computer, on the desk beside it, on my lap, and in the open desk drawer, have kept me company while writing.

Picture acknowledgments

All photography © Octopus Publishing Group/Keith Colin apart from the following:

Alamy 52; Christian Heinrich 69; Helene Rogers 33; Isobel Flynn 7, 122; Juniors Bildarchiv 17; Picture Partners 42; Ray Humphrey 129; tbkmedia.de 14, 133; Tetra Images 34, 163; **Animal Photography** Sally Anne Thompson 146; **Ardea** Jean Michel Labat 121; John Daniels 35, 71, 116; Rolf Kopfle 134; **Corbis** Pat Doyle 115; **DK Images** Jane Burton 143; **Fotolia** bpablo 98; diefotomacher 166; Eric Isselee 123; indeepdark 96; Julijah 137; maja 31; Maja 55; Oliynik Pavlo 152; shocky 149; Simone van den Berg 125; Skv7774 2; wojciechhajduk 58; **Getty Images** 156; Dorling Kindersley 94; GK Hart/Vikki Hart 185; Jane Burton 175; **iStockphoto.com** ImagesbyTrista 80; jorgeantonio 37; photoshopped 39; ajsn 50; Casarsa 28; EEI_Tony 36, 90, 150; Gaussian_Blur 74; ingret 38; jkitan 13; PerlAlexander 23; Photoshopped 26, 126; piemash 130; rafal rzdeb 145; spxChrome 92; suemack 176; SVM 135; **Masterfile** 136, 138, 173, 183; **Nature Picture Library** Aflo 144; Jane Burton 103; **Octopus Publishing Group Limited** 86, 87; Jane Burton 30, 40, 43, 56, 59, 66, 66, 95, 102, 105, 131, 151, 153, 158, 159, 160, 161, 169, 172, 184; **Petsafe** Staywell by petsafe 84; **RSPCA Photolibrary** 117; **Shutterstock** Antonio Jorge Nunes 141; david vadala 171; Efanov Aleksey Anatolievich 16; Eric Isselee 12, 148; graham s. klotz 77; Gregor Kervina 19; ingret 24; Lars Christensen 4, 88, 99; Lein de Leon Yong 120; Magdalena Bujak 68; Mario Savoia 147; Nikolay Titov 119; Pavel Sazonov 15, 73, 78; Ronen 21; Stephen Orsillo 85; Tatiana Lebedeva 81; Tony Campbell 6, 8, 18, 62, 63, 112, 124, 139, 142; Utekhina Anna 65, 75; **Warren Photographic** Jane Burton 1, 10, 51, 60, 64, 76, 82, 91, 127, 154, 165, 187; **Stock.XCHNG** Karolina Przybysz 140; Mikkel Toke Gronkjaer 97.

Executive Editor Trevor Davies

Editor Kerenza Swift

Executive Art Editor Penny Stock

Designers Janis Utton/Nicola Liddiard

Production Manager David Hearn

Picture Library Assistant Ciaran O'Reilly